To Jim
Congr...
Sept 27, 2021
Blessings —
B. Patterson

II Cor 9:8

33

EXCHANGES THROUGH THE SACRIFICE OF JESUS

BILL M PATTERSON

WESTBOW
P R E S S®
A DIVISION OF THOMAS NELSON
& ZONDERVAN

This book is a work of non-fiction. Unless otherwise noted, the author
and the publisher make no explicit guarantees as to the accuracy of
the information contained in this book and in some cases, names of
people and places have been altered to protect their privacy.

WestBow Press books may be ordered through booksellers or by contacting:

WestBow Press
A Division of Thomas Nelson & Zondervan
1663 Liberty Drive
Bloomington, IN 47403
www.westbowpress.com
844-714-3454

Interior images by: Rhonda Lettow & Ryan Elizabeth Ketcher.
Also listed in the bibliography for Illustrations

ISBN: 978-1-6642-3494-9 (sc)
ISBN: 978-1-6642-3493-2 (hc)
ISBN: 978-1-6642-3495-6 (e)

Library of Congress Control Number: 2021910476

Print information available on the last page.

WestBow Press rev. date: 06/14/2021

ACKNOWLEDGMENTS

First, I must thank God, the originator of the *EXCHANGES* offered to us through the sacrifice of Jesus. I thank God for including me and my family in these *Exchanges* that effectively cover every need that we will ever have.

Next, I want to thank the soloist, Carolyn Fleming, who sang the phrase from the song, *I Got the Best of the Trade*. It was indeed this short phrase that began this journey for me.

I thank my illustrators, Rhonda Lettow and Ryan Elizabeth Ketcher, for sharing their artistic gifts, and for being both inspirational and creative.

I thank my teachers at Bible College, especially Robert Girouard and Jacob Regier, for teaching me how to study the Bible in a systematic manner.

Extraordinary kudos from me to my mentor, Derek Prince, who propelled me on this journey of the *Exchanges from the Cross*.

I thank my editors, my wife Vicki, who, for twenty years, taught elementary students how to write in a creative manner, and especially Shay Patterson, a graduate of the University of Chicago and an extraordinary teacher of critical thinking and writing.

I thank my Social Studies professors at West Texas A & M University for taking a very personal interest in me, which resulted in greatly improving my writing ability. You were an important part of God's plan for my life.

With a grateful heart,

Bill M Patterson

INTRODUCTORY REMARKS

33 EXCHANGES THROUGH THE SACRIFICE
OF JESUS BY BILL M PATTERSON

This journey of EXCHANGES in my life began at the age of eighteen. I was listening to a solo on a Sunday morning, sung by a shy girl from Alabama. I was impacted by one phrase in the song: *"I'm sure I got the best of the trade."*

Some years later, I traveled to Southeast Texas to hear the teaching of Derek Prince. He taught on the *Six Exchanges of the Cross.* This teaching would become a vital segment of my journey.

About this time in my life, I began to do a considerable amount of counseling. I soon realized that, as I identified a basic need in an individual's life, there was already in place an EXCHANGE provided by the sacrifice of Jesus.

Soon my list of EXCHANGES grew from six to ten—then twelve—then sixteen. When I could identify twenty EXCHANGES through the sacrifice of Jesus, I decided to list them in a book. However, as I wrote the book, the list grew once again to twenty-four—then twenty-five—then thirty—and now thirty-three.

For me, this has been an extraordinary journey through the Word of God.

It began with a song on a Sunday morning:

> *"I traded my sins for salvation—for a temple to dwell in God made... .*
>
> *Then I got so much more than I had before.*
>
> *Now I'm sure I got the best of the trade."* [1]
>
> *Words and Music by Thomas Dorsey*

CONTENTS

EXCHANGE # 1

MY SINS FOR YOUR REMISSION (ERASURE) OF SINS

THEME SCRIPTURE:

ACTS 10:43— "To Him all of the prophets witness that, through His Name, whoever believes in Him will receive remission of sins." *NKJV*

PETER'S MESSAGE ON THE DAY OF PENTECOST:

ACTS 2:38—"...Repent, and let every one of you be baptized in the Name of Jesus Christ for the remission of sins;..." *NKJV*

ILLUSTRATION:

IN THE LATE 1960S, a certain Youth Evangelist was traveling throughout the USA. After a particularly good service one night, he was confronted by a soldier who had been to Viet Nam. "You said that Jesus died, shedding His blood, so that all who come to Him might be forgiven, and that their sins would be removed. I cannot experience that because I have sinned too much. I have gone too far to be forgiven." The Youth Evangelist explained that Jesus had gone to the very bottom of sins, that no one could ever go beyond His reach. When this spiritual fact was revealed to the young soldier, he gave His life to God, was forgiven, and made Jesus Lord of his life.

REMISSION OF SINS:

THE EXCHANGE:

Jesus took all my sins so that my sins would be erased (remitted).

O T Scriptures prophesied of this:

Psalms 103:12—"For as far as the East is from the West, so far has He removed our transgressions from us." *NIV*

The distance from the East to the West cannot be measured. It is an infinite distance. This merciful action was not possible under the Old Covenant. In the Old Covenant, the sins of the Hebrews were "covered" by the sacrifice of animals for a year, until such time as the High Priest would offer annual sacrifice once again.

NEW COVENANT—NEW MEDIATOR:

However, in the New Covenant, there is a new mediator, Jesus Christ, the Son of God, Who gave himself as the eternal sacrifice for the sins of all humans who would ever live on the Earth. In the New

Covenant, our sins are removed from us, never to be remembered again.

Hebrews 8:6— "But now He has obtained a more excellent ministry, inasmuch as He is also Mediator of a better covenant, which was established on better promises." *NKJV*

I Timothy 2:5— "For there is one God and one Mediator between God and men, the Man Christ Jesus." *NKJV*

PROPHECY OF MICAH:

Micah also prophesied of this New Covenant experience: "...You will cast all our sins into the depths of the sea." *Micah 7:19 NKJV*

COST OF BENEFIT:

Jesus carried every sin, past sins, present sins, and future sins—every sin without exception, so that no one would ever be beyond His reach—beyond His touch. Therefore, Jesus, in that moment when God the Father placed every sin upon Him, became more sinful than any person in the history of humanity.

RESPONSE:

I confess with my mouth that Jesus is Lord. I believe in my heart that God raised Him from the dead. Thank You Lord for taking my sins, so that I could be forgiven. I accept You now as my Savior.

PERSONAL NOTES—EXCHANGE 1:

1. What happens to one's sins when he/she establishes a relationship with God through His Son, Jesus?

_____

_____

_____

2. What is the promise concerning your sins from the prophetic Psalms?

_____

_____

_____

3. What is the cost of this exchange?

_____

_____

_____

_____

4. What was the prophecy of Micah concerning your sins?

_____

_____

_____

_____

EXCHANGE # 2

MY SIN NATURE FOR HIS RIGHTEOUSNESS

THEME SCRIPTURE:

II Corinthians 5:21—"He (God) made Him (Jesus) Who knew no sin to be sin for us, so that **we could become the righteousness of God in Him.**" *NKJV*

ILLUSTRATION:

Karen had grown up in a small Church in the 1970s. Like many churches in that era, her church's teaching involved strict religious rules—no dancing, no movies, no football games, etc. She adopted the church's teaching, and, as a result, became self-righteous and therefore judgmental.

5

During the 1980s, Karen was introduced to the teaching of righteousness. She not only resisted the teaching of righteousness, but she argued against it. She had changed in some of her former beliefs, but simply could not handle this teaching of righteousness.

Karen attended a seminar that featured several international teachers. However, it was the teaching of a Baptist minister that gripped her. It was indeed a teaching on righteousness.

As the minister taught concerning the tremendous price that Jesus paid so that we could be righteous even as He is righteous, the Holy Spirit spoke to her, "you have no right to resist this gift of grace. Jesus paid the cost of 'becoming sin nature' so that you could be righteous."

With tears running down her cheeks, Karen repented and fully accepted the gift of righteousness into her spirit.

TEACHING:

In the beginning, in the Garden of Eden, Adam disobeyed the directive from God: "...Of every tree of the garden, you may freely eat, but of the tree of knowledge of good and evil you shall not eat..." Gen. 2:16-17 *NKJV* When Adam sinned, he lost his unique position with God: he was banned from the Garden; he lost his fellowship with God; he lost his nature of righteousness; his nature became SIN NATURE.

Adam, by his position, father of the human race, passed his sin nature to every human being—to every generation. The one exception was Jesus, who was not born from man's seed, but was born of a virgin by the Holy Spirit. This is the reason that Jesus was born of a virgin, so that He would never have a sin nature until He hung on the cross.

SIN FOR RIGHTEOUSNESS:

"He (God) made Him (Jesus) Who knew no sin to be sin for us, that we might become the righteousness of God in Him. *II Corinthians 5:21 NKJV*

We are no longer sinners—not even "sinners saved by grace". We are new creatures—alive unto God—dead to sin—dead to the instrument of sin.

We are the righteousness of God. That is our new identity in Christ.

THE BENEFITS OF RIGHTEOUSNESS:

"...the effective, fervent prayer of a righteous man avails much." *James 5:16 NKJV*

"For by the one man's offense death reigned through the one, much more those who receive abundance of grace and the gift of righteousness will reign in life through the One, Jesus Christ." *Romans 5:17 NKJV*

"Therefore, brethren, having boldness to enter the Holiest by the blood of Jesus, by a new and living way..." *Hebrews 10:19 NKJV*

We can now approach the presence of God without fear or condemnation. Jesus made the way for us.

NO FEAR IN THE PRESENCE OF GOD:

Because of the work of righteousness in the believer's life, he does not feel condemnation when approaching God. The believer can come "boldly to His throne". *Hebrews 4:16; 10:19 NKJV*

REIGNING IN LIFE:

Romans 5:17—"For if by one man's offense death reigned through the one, much more those who receive abundance of grace and of the gift of righteousness will reign in life, through the One, Jesus Christ." *NKJV*

RIGHTEOUSNESS, A GIFT:

Righteousness is the first "charismata" (gift of grace) listed in the Scriptures.

Charismata=gift of grace—Strong's # 5485=grace; gift. ---(Greek language)-Strong's # 5486=spiritual gifts; spiritual endowments)₂

It is the gift of God. *You cannot earn righteousness. Man's* attempts to be righteous is "as filthy rags" in the sight of God. *Isaiah 64:6 NKJV*

COST OF BENEFIT:

Jesus went to the cross as a righteous man, not having any sin. While hanging on the cross, there came the moment when God changed the nature of Jesus to SIN NATURE. Jesus was identifying with us in every category of need that mankind could ever have. Sin nature is that specific instrument in man/woman that causes man/woman to commit sins. Sin (singular) causes us to commit sins (plural).

When Jesus became SIN, God the Father turned His back on Jesus. Jesus had stated that His very life was His union with the Father. *John Chapter 14 NKJV,* He also stated, "I know that You always hear Me..." *John 11:42 NKJV*

Suddenly, for the very first time in the Earthly life of Jesus, there was silence in Heaven. His cry was, "My God, My God, why have You forsaken Me?" *Matthew 27:46 NKJV* There was no response from

Heaven. From this moment forward in the sacrificial plan, Jesus was totally alone. Sin had separated Him from the Father.

PRAYER:

Thank You, Jesus, for taking my sin nature, so that I could be a new creation, receiving the gift of righteousness. I acknowledge Your gift of righteousness to me, knowing that, through Your exchange, I am no longer a slave to sin. Thank You, Jesus, for paying the ultimate price for me by becoming sin. Help me, Holy Spirit, to be conscious of righteousness, instead of sin. In the mighty Name of Jesus—Amen.

RESPONSE:

1. knowing this...*Romans 6:6 NKJV*
2. counting it done (personalize)...*Romans 6:11 NKJV*
3. *confession: "I am no longer a slave to sin. I am no longer a slave to lust. I am no longer a slave to fear. I am no longer a slave to jealousy. I am no longer a slave to hurts and rejection. I am no longer a slave to discouragement. I am no longer a slave to depression."*

I must understand that I cannot ever earn God's righteousness. It is a gift from God. It is listed in the Greek language as a *charismata*, that is, a gift of grace. In this case, it is the gift of righteousness. When an individual comes to God through Jesus, he/she is converted, born again, and becomes a new creation in Christ Jesus. Immediately, the gift of righteousness is imparted to the new convert.

My response is to believe this promise of the Great Exchange—that God changes my nature from sin nature to the very righteousness of God in Christ.

PERSONAL NOTES—EXCHANGE 2:

1. What gift does God give to us in exchange for our sin-nature?

_____

_____

_____

_____

2. What is the exchange that is listed in *II Corinthians 5:21, NKJV*?

_____

_____

_____

_____

3. Name three benefits of righteousness.

_____

_____

_____

_____

4. How can a Christian earn righteousness?

_____

_____

_____

_____

5. Name the three extraordinary things that God performed that is listed in *Zechariah 12:01, KJV.*

_____

_____

_____

_____

6. List four things that occurs when an individual is "born again".

_____

_____

_____

_____

7. What was the cost of this exchange?

_____

_____

_____

_____

EXCHANGE # 3

MY SPIRITUAL DEATH
FOR HIS SPIRITUAL LIFE

THEME SCRIPTURE:

EPHESIANS 2:01— "As for you, you were dead in your transgressions and sins....because of His great love for us, God, Who is rich in mercy, made us alive with Christ..." *NIV*

ILLUSTRATION:

David was a junior in High School, President of his junior class, and a running back on his school's football team. An evangelist came to David's city for a city-wide crusade. David's coach asked him to attend the crusade one evening.

David thought that this crusade was a waste of his time. He sat through the service with another player from his football team. He wished that he had gone to the Pizza Hut to meet with some of the girls in his class.

The service closed with the evangelist asking for all who had never invited Jesus into their hearts and lives to please come forward. David felt an overwhelming urgency to go forward. A counselor talked with him for a few minutes. They prayed together, and David invited Jesus to be his Savior and Lord. He knew that something significant had happened in his life.

What David thought to be a wasted evening, became the most important night of his life. He was "born again", receiving eternal life.

TEACHING:

NEW BIRTH:

THE spirit within man/woman is quickened—comes alive unto God.

If the spirit in man comes alive, then it must have previously been in a state of death—not alive unto God—spiritually dead. *Ephesians 2:1 NKJV*—"And you He made alive, who were dead in trespasses and sins." You were dead in trespasses and sins. Your spirit was dead to God. There was no fellowship with God—no relationship with Him. All of those conditions change—in a moment of time—instantly—when we come to God through His Son, Jesus.

Contrast of Old Covenant to New Covenant: *NKJV*

Hebrews 9 NKJV

I Peter 1:19—NKJV

YOUR RECREATED SPIRIT:

Pneuma— (Greek word) =spirit—*Strong's # 4151₃*

"...the Lord, Who stretches out the heavens, lays the foundation of the earth, and forms the **spirit of man** within him." *Zechariah 12:01 NKJV*

Another translation reads, "...formed a spirit in the midst of man." *Zechariah 12:1 KJV*

God created man as a spirit being, gave him a soul, and housed him in a body.

He placed man (Adam) in the Garden of Eden and made a companion for him (Eve). God gave Adam dominion over the Earth with one restriction: "...of the tree of the knowledge of good and evil you shall not eat, for in the day that you eat of it, you shall surely die." *Genesis 2:17 NKJV*

Satan entered the garden and deceived Eve, who ate of the forbidden tree. Later, Adam joined her in the disobedience. That very day Adam died in his spirit. His fellowship with God was cut off. He was driven from the garden. His nature was changed from righteousness to a sinful nature.

When Adam sinned, everyone sinned. His sinful nature was inherited by every generation that followed. Paul stated, "For as by one man's disobedience, many were made sinners so also by one Man's obedience, many will be made righteous." *Romans 5:19 NKJV*

NEW BIRTH:

Thus, mankind inherited from Adam a sinful nature and a spirit that was dead in trespasses and sins. "And you He made alive, who were dead in trespasses and sins." *Ephesians 2:1 NKJV*

THE SPIRIT MUST BE BORN AGAIN:

Jesus answered Nicodemus, "Most assuredly I say unto you, unless one is born again, he cannot see the kingdom of God...unless one is born of water and the Spirit, he cannot enter the kingdom of God." *John 3:3-5 NKJV*

THE NEW BIRTH EXPERIENCE:

John 20:22— **"...**He breathed on [them] and said to them, 'Receive (admit) the Holy Spirit.'" *NKJV*

PLEASE NOTE:

While on the cross, Jesus, who knew no sin, was made to be SIN, so that we might be the righteousness of God in Christ. *(2 Corinthians 5:21) KJV* God, in His plan for us, required Jesus, our representative and sacrifice, to take on the sin nature of mankind. Jesus was the sinless, spotless, Lamb of God, who never needed spiritual redemption.

JESUS—OUR PATTERN:

In order for Jesus to identify with us, He had to die. Of course, because we are so connected to our bodies, we immediately think of physical death. However, His spiritual death was much more important for us. When He became SIN (sin nature), He died spiritually. His spirit died. He was identifying with us. If He had not died in His spirit, It would not have been necessary for God to justify Him and raise Him in His spirit. This simply means that God raised Him in His spirit and made Him righteous once again. God restored in Him all that He had lost through the process of identifying with us in our needs.

FROM SPIRITUAL DEATH TO SPIRITUAL LIFE:

Our sin nature would have to be changed to righteousness. This change took place at the exact time that Jesus had fulfilled all of the requirements of God the Father, in order that man could be redeemed and restored to the place that God intended. This "change" is referred to in the Word as "you must be born again". *John 3:03 KJV* His Body of flesh was offered for us because we were the ones who were dead spiritually. When Jesus had finished the assignment of completing all that the PERFECT JUSTICE of God required, God raised Him (Jesus) in His spirit. This is the new birth. Jesus, as our representative, was the first to experience the "new birth". The Word declares that Jesus was the "first-born of many brethren". (*Romans 8:29*) *KJV*

The disciples of Jesus also had to experience the "new birth". I believe that this occurred when Jesus breathed on them and said, "Receive the Holy Spirit". *John 20:22 NKJV* At this point the disciples received spiritual life—they "came alive in their spirits".

NECESSITY OF THE NEW BIRTH EXPERIENCE:

In John, chapter 3, Jesus is speaking to Nicodemus, "Most assuredly, I say to you, unless one is born again, he cannot see the kingdom of God." Nicodemus replied, "How can one be born when he is old? Can he enter a second time into his mother's womb and be born?" Jesus answered, "Most assuredly, I say to you, unless one is born of water and the Spirit, he cannot enter the kingdom of God…" *John 3:3-5 NKJV*

SPIRIT—THE REAL YOU:

Man/woman is a spirit (in the image of God). He/she has a soul (mind, will, emotions). He/she lives in a body. Your body is the house in which you live while you are her on Earth.

TERMS USED IN THE SCRIPTURES:

- The heart
- The hidden man of the heart
- The spirit man
- The inner man

FACTS ABOUT THE SPIRIT OF MAN:

- The Holy Spirit bears witness with our spirit that we have become the Sons of God.
- The born-again Christian receives the Gift of Righteousness, changing his/her nature from sin nature to righteousness.
- The born-again Christian receives the Gift of Eternal Life in his/her spirit.
- The Christian asks for and is baptized in the Holy Spirit.
- The Christian receives the fruit of the Spirit in his/her spirit.
- The born-again spirit of the believer is in agreement with the Holy Spirit and the Word of God.
- The born-again spirit of the believer must express himself/herself through his/her soul. This fact should motivate the believer to be transformed in his/her soul.

HOW CAN ANYONE BE BORN AGAIN?

Anyone can be born again (saved) by making Jesus the Savior and Lord of his/her life. This takes place through belief and confession.

"If you confess with your mouth that Jesus is Lord and believe in your heart that God has raised Him from the dead, you shall be saved (born-again). For with the heart, one believes unto righteousness and with the mouth confession is made unto salvation." *Romans 10:9-10 NKJV*

COST OF THIS EXCHANGE:

When Jesus became SIN nature, God the Father turned His back on Jesus. Jesus had stated that His very life was His union with the Father. He also stated, "I know that You always hear Me." *John 11:42 NKJV*

Suddenly, for the very first time in the Earthly life of Jesus, there was silence in Heaven. His cry was, "My God, why have You forsaken Me?" *Matthew 27:46 NKJV* There was no response from Heaven. From this moment forward in the sacrificial plan, Jesus was totally alone. Sin had separated Him from the Father.

MY RESPONSE:

1. Confess with your mouth that Jesus is Lord.
2. Believe in your heart that God raised Jesus from the dead.
3. Declare, "I receive You, Jesus, into my life."
4. Thank Him for forgiving your sins.

PRAYER TO BE BORN AGAIN:

Father God, I confess with my mouth that Jesus is Lord and I believe in my heart that You raised Him from the dead. I ask You to be my God and I ask You, Jesus, to be my Savior and my Lord. I thank You for loving me and coming to Earth to die in my place. I receive You now as my Savior—in the Name of Jesus, my Lord, I pray. Amen.

PERSONAL NOTES—CHAPTER 3

1. What happens to a person's spirit when he/she is "born again"?

   _____

   _____

   _____

   _____

2. What is the exchange listed in *Ephesians 2:01, NIV*?

   _____

   _____

   _____

   _____

3. Describe the "real you" according to this author.

   _____

   _____

   _____

   _____

4. What terms are used in the Scriptures to indicate the spirit of man/woman?

   _____

   _____

   _____

   _____

5. List seven facts about the spirit of man.

_____

_____

_____

_____

6. What was the cost for this exchange?

_____

_____

_____

_____

7. What should be the response of an individual, in order to be born again?

_____

_____

_____

_____

EXHANGE # 4

MY SINNING AS A CHRISTIAN FOR HIS FORGIVENESS

THEME SCRIPTURE:

I John 1:9— "If we confess our sins, He is faithful and just to forgive us our sins, and to cleanse us from all unrighteousness." *NKJV*

ILLUSTRATION:

Georgia was born into a Christian family in the South. When she was eleven years of age, she attended a Christian camp for kids. One evening at the close of the service, an invitation was given to those kids who had never accepted Jesus as their Savior. Georgia felt the need to respond, and immediately went forward and received Jesus as her Savior. She experienced the cleansing power of the blood of

Jesus and knew that there had been a change in her life. At the end of the camp, she was baptized.

A year later, Georgia attended a Christian camp once again. Throughout the week of camp, she felt that she had not always lived a Christian life. In fact, she knew that at times she had sinned. As a result, Georgia once again went forward at the close of a service, confessed her sins, and received Jesus as her Savior. She was baptized in the lake for a second time.

This experience has been shared by thousands of kids at summer camps. One girl testified that she had been baptized five times at summer camps. This is not a matter of wrong teaching. It is the result of a lack of the correct teaching.

We as Christians who sin have the privilege of confessing our sins and immediately receiving the forgiveness of God the Father. We do not lose our salvation, but we do need to confess our sins, admitting that we messed up.

TEACHING:

I John 1:09— "If we confess our sins, He is faithful and just to forgive us our sins and to cleanse us from all unrighteousness." NKJV

Jesus not only took our sins that we committed before we first came to God, but also the sins that we commit as Christians. John reveals to Christians the solution in the Scripture in *I John 1:09. NKJV*

This promise was written to Christians. It is apparent throughout *I John*, *II John*, and *III John* that the writer is definitely speaking to Christians.

What happens to the Christian who sins? Do all of the sins of one's past return and become a burden for the Christian who commits a sin? When one initially comes to God through the sacrifice of Jesus, all sins are removed. Those sins are purged from one's life and never shall return. They are never remembered by God.

I John 2:01 NKJV— "My little children, these things I write to you, so that you may not sin. And if anyone sins, we have an Advocate with the Father, Jesus Christ the righteous."

THE COST OF THIS EXCHANGE:

As Jesus hung on the cross, God placed all of my sins and all of your sins upon Him. Until this moment, Jesus was without sin. He never committed one sin. So, the sinless One accepted this role of His sacrifice by taking our sins—in fact, He took all of the sins of mankind. He took the sins that I committed before I became a Christian, AND He also took the sins that I would commit after I became a Christian. This means that when you or I sin as Christians, that Jesus has already paid the price for those specific sins. This is also covered by the sacrifice of Jesus.

John writes to Christians in His letter "so that you may not sin." However,"if anyone sins, we have an advocate (lawyer) with the Father, Jesus Christ the righteous." *I John 2:1 NKJV* Jesus, your lawyer, defends you and me, pleading our case in the Court of Mercy and Grace, based upon the fact that He has already taken the very sin that we committed as a Christian.

MY RESPONSE:

The Holy Spirit is committed to your success as a Christian. If you sin, He will very quietly and effectively convict you of your specific sin. Your response should be immediate. However, the temptation will be to delay that confession. Satan will attempt to convince you that you need to suffer—to separate yourself from the fellowship of Christians. You may say to yourself, "I am not worthy to be around Christians right now. I will wait until I am better." In so doing, you will limit your effectiveness for God.

"Father, I confess that I have sinned. I now receive Your cleansing through the blood of Your Son, Jesus Christ. I receive Your forgiveness and Your cleansing from all unrighteousness. I thank You, Jesus, for taking this sin, so I could be free from sin and all unrighteousness."

PERSONAL NOTES—CHAPTER 4

1. What must be the response, towards God, of Christians who sin?

2. What is the exchange listed in *I John 1:09, NKJV*?

3. What was the cost of this exchange?

4. What is the Holy Spirit's commitment to Christians who sin?

5. What is God's response to the Christian who confesses his/her sins?

_____

_____

_____

_____

EXCHANGE # 5

MY CURSE FOR HIS BLESSING

Jesus became the curse so that I could be blessed.

THEME SCRIPTURE:

Galatians 3:13-14— "Christ has redeemed us from the curse of the law, having become a curse for us (for is written, 'cursed is everyone who hangs on a tree') that the blessing of Abraham might come upon the Gentiles in Christ Jesus…" *NKJV*

Genesis 24:01— "Now Abraham was old, well advanced in age, and the Lord had blessed him in all things." *NKJV* This is the type of blessing that is available through this Exchange.

ILLUSTRATION:

The young minister encountered a teenager named Robert on the streets of a large Southwest Texas city. The minister questioned Robert about his life and his goals.

Robert explained his life by the examples of his family. "My mother is in prison. My dad is in prison. My older brother is in prison. My uncle is in prison. My grandfather is in prison. And soon I will be in prison myself."

The minister shared the plan of salvation with the young man, who accepted Jesus and was forgiven of his sins. Then the minister did something that surprised Robert. He commanded the demons to come out of Robert. Robert was freed from the generational curse that had affected all of his family members.

Robert did not go to prison. Robert became a minister.

TEACHING:

If you are committed to living God's way and giving Him the praise and the glory for your successes, then you need to expect His blessings to fill your life. No matter how fast you travel down the road of life, God's blessings will overtake you.

HOW DOES GOD BLESS YOU?

- God will set you on high. *Deuteronomy 28:01; NKJV*
- God will open to you His good treasure. *Deut. 28:12; NKJV*
- God will bless all the work of your hands. *Deut. 28:12; NKJV*
- God will grant you plenty of goods. Deut. *28:11; NKJV*
- God will grant you the increase of your livestock. *Deut. 28:11 NKJV*

- ;God will grant you the increase of the produce of your land. *Deut. 28:11 NKJV*
- God will cause you to be above and not beneath. *Deut. 28:13 NKJV*
- God will cause your enemies who rise against you to be defeated. *Deut. 28:07; NKJV*
- God will command the blessing on you in your storehouses. *Deut. 28:08 NKJV*

WHERE DOES GOD BLESS YOU?

- Blessed shall you be in the city. *Deut. 28:03; NKJV*
- Blessed shall you be in the country. *Deut. 28:03; NKJV*
- Blessed shall you be when you come in. *Deut. 28:06; NKJV*
- Blessed shall you be when you go out. *Deut. 28:06. NKJV*

BLESSINGS OR CURSES?

There are fourteen verses in the 28th chapter of Deuteronomy that deal with the blessing of God. In contrast, there are forty-eight verses that deal with the curses of our enemy, the Devil. Which is going to be better for you?

GENERATIONAL CURSES:

"The sins of the fathers shall be passed on to even the 3rd and 4th generations." *Numbers 14:18 NKJV* In some cases, individuals inherit the tendencies of their ancestors—for example, the son or grandson of an alcoholic might have a tendency to drink to excess. The daughter of a parent or grandparent who experienced Alzheimer's disease may inherit the tendency for that disease. A person might inherit the tendency of a parent or grandparent to experience excessive anger or rage. These tendencies and all other generational curses must be recognized and then delivered by the blood of Jesus and the Name of Jesus. "He/she whom the Son sets free is free indeed." *John 8:36 NIV*

COST OF THIS BENEFIT:

Simply by hanging on the cross, Jesus became a curse. "...Cursed is everyone that hangs on a cross..." *Galatians 3:13 KJV*

RESPONSE:

- Thank the Lord for becoming the curse for you, so that you can enjoy His blessings.
- Be advised that the goal of your enemy, the devil, is to convince you that some of the curses belong to you.
- Know this: "For the laws of the Spirit of life in Christ Jesus has made me free from the law of sin and death." *Romans 8:02 NKJV*
- Choose to live God's way and enjoy His blessings. Throughout the Bible, there are conditions to the blessings that God offers to us. God is the source of every good and perfect gift.

PERSONAL NOTES—CHAPTER 5

1. What is the exchange listed in *Galatians 3:13, NKJV?*

   _____

   _____

   _____

   _____

2. Name five ways in which God blesses us.

   _____

   _____

   _____

   _____

3. Name four places where God blesses us.

   _____

   _____

   _____

   _____

4. What is the cost of this benefit?

   _____

   _____

   _____

   _____

5. What should be the response of the believer to this exchange offer?

    _____

    _____

    _____

    _____

EXCHANGE # 6

THE "OLD ME" FOR THE NEW MAN

THEME SCRIPTURE:

Romans 6:6— "Knowing this, that our old man was crucified with Him, that the body of sin might be done away with, that we should no longer be slaves of sin." *NKJV*

NEW MAN—OTHER TITLES:

The hidden man of the heart;

The inner man;

The spirit man.

EXCHANGE:

The OLD MAN was a sinner. He was the sin nature in me. However, he was nailed to the cross with Jesus. He was executed—killed. As a result, I am no longer a sinner. In the present tense, I am not a sinner saved by grace, I am, instead, a new man—a righteous person—a man whose sins have been removed—a man who has exchanged his sin nature for God's righteousness. "I am a new creation"-created in Christ Jesus. *II Corinthians 5:17 NKJV*

TO WHAT END?

"…that we should no longer be slaves to sin, for when a man/woman dies, he/she is freed from sin." *Romans 6:06-07 NKJV*

JACK TAYLOR REFERENCE:

Jack Taylor, the International Bible teacher, gave the following example in a seminar that I attended in the 1970s: "George was always sinning. His wife would leave their house in the evening to attend a local church. When she returned home, George would curse her, make fun of her religion, and often beat her. George was sinning. He would be both drunk and high on drugs. One evening, upon her return, she entered the house with great trepidation, wondering what George would do. However, George was not sinning. The drugs were present. The alcohol was present. But George was not doing drugs nor drinking. George did not curse her nor beat her, because George was dead."4

A dead man is no longer a slave to sin. *Romans. 6:6 NKJV*

ILLUSTRATION: FROM PERSONAL EXPERIENCE:

The old Bill Patterson was a sinner, dominated by sin, having a sin nature. However, the old Bill Patterson was crucified with Christ, nailed to his cross, so that the new Bill Patterson would not be a slave to sin.

A few years ago, I lived in a small city in the Panhandle of Oklahoma. One evening a stranger drove into my driveway, exited his car, and approached my front door. I met him at the door. He was overjoyed to see me. He said, "I have searched for you for a long time. My job is to deliver this document to you personally." I looked at the letter and replied, "I can't accept this document. I am not that man. He once lived here, but he is gone and will not return."

After the man had left, I thought, "that was an example of what God did for us through Jesus." The old man used to live here in me—in my earthly house. However, he is gone—dead—crucified with Christ, and he will not be back.

Satan comes to the believer with all kinds of messages: messages of hurt, messages of rejection, messages of fear, messages of intimidation, messages of condemnation. He will announce to you: "these messages belong to you—your name is on them." The believer must reply: "I will not receive your messages. They belong to the old man. I am the new man—a new creation—all things are new—all things are of God. The old man no longer lives here. He has died—He has been crucified with Christ. Therefore, he will not be back. I refuse to accept your messages."

35

Therefore, since we, as believers, are no longer slaves to sin, do not let sin reign in your mortal bodies. *Romans. 6:7, 12 NKJV*

COST OF THIS EXCHANGE:

Jesus became sin nature: "God made Him (Jesus) to be SIN, so that we could become the righteousness of God in Christ." *II Corinthians 5:21 NKJV*

As He became sin nature, He was also representing the *old man*. He could only crucify the old man by hanging on the cross Himself.

RESPONSE:

1. KNOWING THIS: the Christian MUST know this! *Romans 6:06 NKJV*
2. PERSONALIZE IT—COUNT IT DONE IN YOUR LIFE. *Romans 6:11 NKJV*
3. REFUSE SATAN'S MESSAGES. (Example of Jesus tempted by Satan in the wilderness).

4. PRAYER:

Thank you, Father, for dealing with, not only the sins that I committed and would commit, but also for dealing with my tendency to commit sins. Thank you for the revelation that my "old man" was crucified with Christ, nailed to His cross, so that I would no longer be a slave to sin. I will no longer accept the messages that Satan sends to me by special delivery. The "old me" no longer lives here. The new man lives here now in this earthly body. The "old me" will not be back. Therefore Satan, I will no longer accept your messages. I am free from sin—free from fear—free from depression—free from discouragement—free from the inheritance of Adam—free in my life in Jesus.

PERSONAL NOTES—CHAPTER 6

1. What is the exchange listed in *Romans 6:06, NKJV*?

_____

_____

_____

_____

2. Name 3 three titles that correspond to the "new man".

_____

_____

_____

_____

3. Name the three component parts of the Christian's response to this exchange.

_____

_____

_____

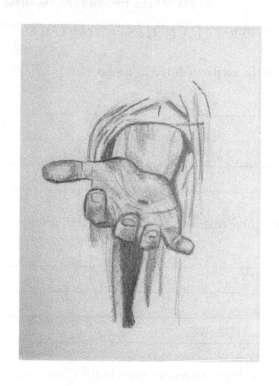

EXCHANGE # 7

MY SICKNESSES. DISEASES, AND PHYSICAL WEAKNESSES FOR HIS HEALING

Jesus took all my sicknesses and diseases in exchange for His healing.

THEME SCRIPTURE:

"Who Himself bore our sins in His own body on the tree, that we, having died to sin might live for righteousness—by whose (wounds) stripes you were healed." *I Peter 2:24 NKJV*

ILLUSTRATION:

Many years ago, there was a healing clinic being conducted in a church in the Southeast part of the US. One evening, at the end of the healing service, a mother and daughter entered the building. The message of healing was new to them. They were frightened concerning what might happen.

However, the daughter had an incurable blood disease. This disease required them to travel hundreds of miles every 3 weeks, so that she could receive treatment at a hospital known for its cancer treatments.

Most of the crowd had already left by the time they entered the church building. The mother and daughter approached the stage, hesitant and frightened.

The daughter faced the minister with her right arm behind her back. He reached for her arm—she resisted. He said to her, "peace—it will be alright. God will heal you tonight."

Then the minister saw her right arm, it was covered with angry red spots, the size of half-dollars. He reassured her, "God is healing you tonight." Then we all prayed.

Tests that week at the medical center revealed that healing had indeed occurred. They could find no evidence that the blood disease had ever been in her body. The damage that had been caused in her body because of the disease had been cleansed—erased—it was gone. Praise the Lord.

SATAN—THE AUTHOR OF REBELLION IN HEAVEN:

"How are you fallen from Heaven, O Lucifer, Son of the morning! *How* you are cut down to the ground." *Isaiah 14:12 NKJV*

"You who weakened the nations! You said in your heart, 'I will ascend to Heaven; I will exalt my throne above the stars of God; I will sit upon the mount of assembly in the uttermost north; I will ascend above the heights of the clouds, I will make myself like the Most High." *Isaiah 14:13-14 NKJV*

SATAN FELL LIKE LIGHTNING FROM HEAVEN:

Jesus told His disciples of His memory concerning Lucifer's (Satan's) rebellion: "I saw Satan fall like lightening from Heaven." *Luke 10:18 NKJV* This event gives us a true contrast between the power of God and the power of Satan.

SATAN THE AUTHOR OF SIN, SICKNESS, DEATH:

Many Bible teachers have referred to Satan as "the author of sin, sickness, and death." *John 10:10 KJV* In other words, these evil attributes did not exist until the rebellion of Heaven and the successful temptation by Satan in the Garden of Eden.

MOTIVE OF SATAN:

Jesus gave the contrast between Himself and Satan: "The thief comes only to steal, kill, and destroy; I have come that they (mankind) might have life, and that they might have it more abundantly." *John 10:10 KJV*

Satan's motive concerning every man, woman, boy, and girl is to keep them from coming to know Jesus as their Lord and Savior. If he fails to accomplish this, he will then send his agents to attempt, on every hand, to restrain them from becoming what God intended and to restrain them from doing that which God purposed for them.

TYPES OF SICKNESSES:

• **Physical sicknesses** are attacks on the health of the bodies of men and women, designed to rob them of that which God intended.

• **Mental sicknesses** are a category of sickness that can range from mental incapacity to simply wrong thinking. God said to His Old Covenant people, "My thoughts are higher than yours." He was saying, "You don't think like I think." Most Christians need healing of the mind because they have never submitted their minds to the Word of God. The Word of God reveals the thoughts of God and the intention of God for His people.

• **Emotional sickness**—Emotions generally have a habit of acting and feeling in whatever manner that they are accustomed. They (emotions) always want to go their own way. Our lives and relationships are too important to allow our emotions to dictate to us how we react to God and to those whom we love. Therefore, emotions must be dealt with aggressively, that is, they must be reined in—much like the reins on a wild stallion. They must not be allowed to run free. Emotional sickness can be caused by hurts, rejections, and disappointments that lead to discouragement and oppression by the agents of Satan.

GOOD NEWS: God has a plan of healing for every type of sickness, disease, and pain.

WAYS IN WHICH HEALING OCCURS:

1. **God's prescription for healing:** *Proverbs 4:20-22 NKJV*

- "Give attention to My words.
- Incline your ear to My sayings.
- Do not let them depart from your eyes.
- Keep them in the midst of your heart.

For they are life to all who find them and they are health to all their flesh."

2. **Basis for healing:**

- *I Peter 2:24 NKJV:* "Himself bore our sins in His own body on the tree, that we, having died to sins, might live for righteousness— by whose stripes you were healed."
  Jesus became our substitute, in that he identified and even experienced every sin, every sickness, every pain, and every weakness that we would ever have. This is the plan of God—that He would put upon Jesus all of our sins and all of our diseases and all of our pains. We do not receive healing because of our goodness or good deeds. We receive healing because we simply believe His Word and thank God for the healing.

3. **Healing through deliverance:**

- On occasion, Jesus expelled the "spirit of infirmity" from individuals. In these cases, an agent of Satan has attacked an individual with a specific sickness, and the healing required that the demon be expelled. When the demon had been expelled, the sickness was gone also.
- On a personal note: In a "healing clinic" that I was teaching, a woman came at the end of the service for prayer for healing.

She complained of a constant pain in her shoulder. The Holy Spirit spoke to me, indicating that it was a spirit of infirmity. I asked her, "whom do you need to forgive?" She began to weep and named the person toward whom she had unforgiveness. She forgave the person in the Name of Jesus, on the basis that Jesus had taken the offense, so that she would not have to bear it. Immediately, the pain left. The spirit of infirmity no longer had a right to be there, so he had to leave and take the pain with him.

4. **GIFTS OF HEALINGS:**

- When the gift of healings is present, the gift of faith will also be present. God gives extraordinary faith to the believer who operates in a specific area of healing. Often times the gift of healings will be directed through a believer for a specific type of sickness or disease.

- For a period of time, in a certain Church, we had all of the ingredients for healing and miracles. There was a real spirit of praise in all of the services. There were believers present who were committed to the ministry of healing. The Holy Spirit orchestrated the happenings. When the sick and diseased came for healing, believers came also, ready to minister. As the believers laid hands on the sick, I declared that the Name of Jesus was above every name, including the name of cancer. In that moment, every ingredient needed was present and healings occurred. Over a period of time, it seemed that every cancer patient received complete deliverance, as confirmed later by the medical community. **The GIFT of HEALING** was definitely present. It was accompanied by the **GIFT of FAITH.**

5. **Healing through the Gift of Faith:**

- The gift of faith works together with the gifts of healing and the working of miracles. This operation of the Holy Spirit is similar to the gift of tongues (other languages) working with the interpretation of tongues (other languages).

- God allows for signs to follow those who believe, so that we can understand and achieve the ministry of healing and the working of miracles. God gives to us, through the Holy Spirit, the gift of faith. This is extraordinary faith. God gives to us His own faith. That should be explosive knowledge for all of us.

6. **Healing through Special Miracles:**

- Aprons and handkerchiefs were taken from the body of Paul and administered to the sick and diseased as God wrought special miracles at the hand of Paul. There are, evidently, normal miracles and special miracles. In other words, there are degrees of miracles. There have been a few through the ages who seemed to have an unusual anointing for special miracles: Paul; Peter; E W Kenyon; John Lake; Kathyrn Kulman; Oral Roberts. Now the number of believers who seem to have that unusual anointing is growing rapidly around the world. Glory be to God in the highest.

CONCLUSION:

It is always God's will to heal. However, not everyone is healed in the same manner. God has a plan of healing for every individual.

The anointing breaks the yoke, including the yoke of sickness, disease, and pain.

COST OF THIS EXCHANGE:

Jesus was made sick with our sicknesses. He was diseased by our diseases. His body was torn apart by the sicknesses, diseases, and pains of the entire world. This was the cost that Jesus paid for our healing.

SCRIPTURE: *I PETER 2:24: NKJV*— "…by His stripes (wounds) you were healed."

RESPONSE:

If I have a pain or a sickness in my body, I will ask myself, "why am I enduring this malady when I know that Jesus has already taken care of this very pain or sickness, so that I would not have to endure it."

PERSONAL NOTES—CHAPTER 7

1. What happened to Satan (Lucifer) when he led a rebellion in Heaven?

   _____

   _____

   _____

   _____

2. How did sin, sickness, and death become a part of the human experience?

   _____

   _____

   _____

   _____

3. What is always the motive of Satan towards human beings?

   _____

   _____

   _____

   _____

4. Name three ways in which healing occurs.

   _____

   _____

   _____

   _____

5. What was the cost for this exchange?

_____

_____

_____

_____

6. What should be the response of one who experiences pain or sickness?

_____

_____

_____

_____

EXCHANGE # 8

MY RELIGIOUS RULES FOR HIS GRACE

THEME SCRIPTURE:

"For the Law was given through Moses, but grace and truth came through Jesus Christ." *John 1:17 KJV*

ILLUSTRATION:

It was the custom of the third-year Latin students at my high school to arrive early for the 9:00 am class. This gave us the opportunity to have discussions. One morning I introduced the subject of religious rules. Each student described the "rules" of his/her denomination. The Baptist students were expected to refrain from drinking, smoking, and dancing. The Catholic students were required to attend Mass every weekend. If they missed Mass, they were required to go to

Confessional and obey the prescribed instructions. In addition, they were taught to marry only those who were Catholics and raise their children in the Catholic Church. The Church of Christ students were required to attend a church which was named the "Church of Christ", and take communion every Sunday. If they missed, they would receive a call or a visit from one of the Elders. The Seventh Day Adventists had to attend church services on Saturday, and keep The Law (Old Covenant). Also, they did not observe Christmas or birthday celebrations. The Pentecostal girls could not wear jeans or pants, must refrain from wearing make-up and jewelry, and be modest in all things (long dresses). Also, the guys and girls alike could not attend dances, could not drink or smoke.

Some of these religious rules are excellent rules and certainly understandable, however, there was such an emphasis on the rules that some of us missed the message of grace. Many of us in that class, regardless of the denomination affiliation, grew up "under law" instead of under grace.

TEACHING:

"The Law came through Moses, but grace and truth came through Jesus Christ" *John 1:17 NKJV*

"In that He says, 'a new covenant', He has made the first covenant obsolete."

Hebrews 8:13 NKJV

JESUS NAILED THE DOCUMENTS OF THE LAW TO HIS CROSS:

"Having wiped out the handwriting of requirements (the Law) that was against us. And He has taken it out of the way, having nailed it to the cross." *Colossians 2:14 NKJV*

"Let no man judge you in food or in drink, or regarding feast days or a new moon or sabbaths." *Colossians 2:16 NKJV*

DEFINITION FROM OLD TESTAMENT:

Covenant—Hebrew word—beriyth—Strong's # 1285—meaning "to cut"; covenant (made from passing between two pieces of flesh).5

DEFINITION FROM NEW TESTAMENT:

Covenant: Greek word—diatheke—meaning testament; covenant; contract. Strong's Concordance # 1242.6

HISTORY OF COVENANT:

ABRAHAM cut covenant with a few of his neighbors before the Covenant with God.

Traditional history among the ancient tribes in Africa and the Middle East revealed that covenant was a common practice, although the covenants that were made were not at all common in nature. Covenant was the most serious of legal and relational events among all the tribes.

Missionaries such as Livingston and Stanley used covenant with tribal chiefs to introduce the gospel to certain tribes in Africa. The early missionaries to Africa all declared that they had never known of a blood covenant being broken. This was a sacred rite among all the primitive tribes.

TRIBAL METHOD USED FOR BLOOD COVENANT:

- An incision is made in the wrist or finger.
- The participants of the covenant touch the incisions together.
- The blood from each participant mingles together.
- Promises are stated aloud.
- Curses are pronounced on any participant who breaks the covenant.

RESULTS OF A COVENANT:

- Enemies become friends.
- No one takes advantage of the other.
- The covenant cannot be eradicated or cancelled.
- Everything that each owns becomes available to the other if needed.
- Children of the 3rd and 4th generations honor the covenant.
- Memorials are arranged (such as the planting of a tree) to remind everyone of the covenant.7

This understanding of Covenant, especially the New Covenant, elevates the meaning and significance of what God did for us through His Son, Jesus.

OLD COVENANT:

- This was a blood covenant between God and Abraham.
- This covenant was renewed through Moses.
- The guarantee of the covenant on man's part was the cutting of flesh (circumcision) The guarantee of the covenant on God's part was the Name of God.

- "By Myself I have sworn." *Genesis 22:16 NKJV; Isaiah 45:23 NKJV*
- Later, God gave them the Law of the Covenant.
- God promised to be their protector, their sustainer, their healer, their God.

NEW COVENANT:

- This covenant made the Old Covenant obsolete. *Hebrews 10:09 NKJV*
- This covenant is based on the Grace of God.
- Jesus was the blood offering—the eternal sacrifice for the covenant.
- Jesus is the High Priest of our confessions.
- Jesus represented our part in the covenant—He was our substitute.
- This covenant contains exceedingly great and precious promises. *II Peter 1:3-4 KJV*
- Jesus is the guarantor (surety) of the New Covenant. *Hebrews 7:22 NKJV*

THE IMPORTANCE OF GRACE:

Every spiritual experience, every spiritual blessing, and every spiritual gift comes by grace through faith. GRACE cannot be earned. However, Jesus paid the tremendous cost for the grace of God. That grace is dispensed to you by the Holy Spirit.

DEFINITION OF GRACE:

GRACE is that invisible power that empowers you to be what otherwise you could not be.

Grace is that invisible power that empowers you to do what otherwise you could not do.

Grace is that invisible power that empowers you to receive what otherwise you could not receive.

COST OF THIS BENEFIT:

Jesus had to leave His position in Heaven, come down to Earth as a human, and give His life, shedding His precious blood for the redemption of our sins.

RESPONSE:

Thank You, Lord, for coming to bring to me a new and better covenant. I repent of trying to live for You by keeping religious rules established by men. I commit to You to move and live and have my very being in the New Covenant—that is, Your grace and Your truth.

PERSON NOTES—CHAPTER 8

1. What did Jesus do to the documents of the Law?

_____

_____

_____

2. List seven things concerning the New Covenant.

_____

_____

_____

_____

3. Explain the importance of grace to every Christian.

_____

_____

_____

_____

4. List the three enabling powers that grace provides to the Christian.

_____

_____

_____

_____

5. What was the cost of this benefit?

_____

_____

_____

_____

EXCHANGE # 9

MY DEPRESSION FOR HIS GARMENT OF PRAISE

THEME SCRIPTURE:

Isaiah 61:3—"...the Lord has anointed Me...to give ...the garment of praise for the spirit of heaviness..." *NKJV*

ILLUSTRATION:

King Saul, infested with demons, would call for David to come and play the harp for him, so that the depression would be driven away.

James could not remember very many times in his life that he was not aware of an extraordinary sense of oppression. His father had left him and his mother when James was 11 years old. His mother, being an alcoholic, was drunk every night. She would often curse James and physically abuse him.

Strangely, his mother played gospel music in the home. Among the many CDs that his mother played, there were two ladies who sang beautifully. Anytime that James heard one of these ladies sing, he felt relief from his oppression. The anointed music gave him hope.

TEACHING:

PRAISE ACTIVATES THE WEAPON OF THE NAME OF JESUS:

Psalms 8:1-3 NKJV: "O Lord, our Lord, how excellent is Your name in all the Earth! You have set Your glory above the Heavens. Out of the mouth of babes and unweaned infants, You have established strength because of Your foes (enemies), that You might silence the enemy and the avenger."

PLEASE NOTE:

- The Psalmist was speaking about the Name of the Lord.
- God established a special strength for His children.
- The strength that God established was so powerful that it silences the enemy.
- God's people need to discover this source of strength.

Matthew 21:15-16 records the event that involved the children in the porches and courts of the temple crying out, "Hosanna to the Son of David". The chief priests and the scribes were indignant toward Jesus, and said to Him, "Do you hear what these are saying?"

And Jesus replied to them, "Yes, have you never read, 'Out of the mouths of children and infants You have perfected praise'?" *NKJV*

Jesus was not merely quoting the Psalm; He was giving a revelation—identifying the source of strength that silences the enemy—namely praise that glorifies or lifts up the Name of Jesus.

Summary—*Psalms 8; Matthew 21:15-16: NKJV*

- The Psalmist was singing about the Name of the Lord.
- The source of strength was praise toward the name of the Lord.
- When believers (God's children) praise the Name of the Lord, the enemy is silenced.
- The enemy who is the accuser of the brethren needs to be silenced.
- In this type of atmosphere, miracles often happen, because faith is not contaminated or diluted by thoughts of unbelief or unworthiness that come from the enemy [because he is silenced].

PERSONAL EXPERIENCE:

In the 1980s, Vicki and Bill Patterson, with a few friends, for the first time knowingly used praise to launch the mighty weapon—the Name of Jesus. As a result, people who came to our church with needs did not have to struggle and fight with words of doubt and unbelief, because Satan, the enemy, and accuser, was silenced within that gathering. Therefore, there were many miracles, many healings of terminal diseases, and many signs and wonders—to God be the glory.

NOTES ON PRAISE:

The meaning of the word "Psalms" is praise. The *Book of Psalms* is a book of praises to the Lord. Because of the *Book of Psalms*, we can praise the Lord intelligently, knowing that we are praising the Lord according to His Word.

WHEN SHOULD WE PRAISE?

The Psalmist declared, "I will bless the Lord at all times—his praise shall continually be in my mouth. My soul shall make its boast in the Lord..." *Psalms 34:1-2 NKJV*

The decision of the Psalmist was to bless or praise the Lord at all times. Then he invites us to join him. "O magnify the Lord **with me** and **let us** exalt his name **together**." *Psalms 34:3 NKJV*

WHO SHOULD PRAISE THE LORD?

- "Let everything that has breath praise the Lord." *Psalms 150:6 NKJV*
- "The dead do not praise the Lord." *Psalms 115:17 NKJV*

HOW SHOULD WE PRAISE?

- By "singing psalms and hymns and spiritual songs—making melody in your heart to the Lord." *Ephesians 5:19* KJV
- "O clap your hands all you people—shout unto God with a voice of triumph.*" Psalms 47:1 KJV*
- "I will lift my heart with my hands to the God of the Heavens." *Lamentations 3:41 KJV*
- I will praise the Lord in the Spirit and with understanding; *I Cor. 14:15; KJV*
- "Let my evening sacrifice be the lifting up of my hands..." *Psalms 141:2 KJV*
- "I will praise You with my whole heart" *Psalms 138:01 KJV*

- "Because Your lovingkindness is better than life, my lips shall praise You...I will lift up my hands in Your Name." *Psalms 63:3-4 KJV*
- "...let us continually offer the sacrifice of praise to God—that is the fruit of our lips—giving thanks to His Name." *Hebrews 13:15 KJV*

RESPONSE:

I commit to the Lord, on behalf of myself, my family, and my friends to be an encourager. I will fill my home and my vehicle with praise music that will inspire and uplift me. Because of this commitment, I will be better for Him and better for my family and my friends.

"I will bless the Lord at all times—His praise shall continually be in my mouth. My soul shall make her boast in the Lord...*Psalms 34:1-4 KJV* I will magnify the Lord. I will praise His Name forever. He is my Rock—my Fortress—my deliverer. I praise the Name of the Lord."

PERSONAL NOTES—CHAPTER 9

1. What is the exchange that is listed in *Isaiah 61:03, NKJV*?

    _____

    _____

    _____

    _____

2. What is one of the ways in which the Name of Jesus is activated as a weapon against Satan?

    _____

    _____

    _____

    _____

3. Who should be the ones who praise the Lord?

    _____

    _____

    _____

    _____

4. Name six ways in which a Christian can praise the Lord.

    _____

    _____

    _____

    _____

5. When should Christians praise the Lord?

_____

_____

_____

_____

EXCHANGE # 10

MY OPPRESSION FOR HIS LIBERTY

MY ADDICTION FOR HIS DELIVERANCE;

MY IMPRISONMENT FOR HIS FREEDOM.

THEME SCRIPTURE:

Luke 4:18—"The Spirit of the Lord is upon Me, because He has anointed Me to....proclaim liberty to those who are oppressed..." *NKJV*

ILLUSTRATION:

Della, a fifteen-year-old girl, lived with her single mother in the Southeast part of the US. She had been in trouble repeatedly with the local police, beginning when she was twelve years old. Her mother had sought help for her from every source available. Della simply cursed those who attempted to help her.

Finally, the mother, helpless and hopeless, threw Della out of her home, and told her she was not to return.

Della was homeless. She was immediately befriended by a young man, who offered her a place to stay. He offered her a drug to make her feel better. She was immediately under the influence of a powerful drug. The man then called his friends to come to his house. In the next seven days and nights, Della was gang-raped and physically and mentally abused. She was then turned out once again to the streets.

The impact of this experience enraged Della. She was "oppressed" by rejection, rebellion, and rage. For the next four years, she wandered from city to city in search of relief.

When she was nineteen, she wandered into a hotel lobby. There was a Christian seminar being held in that hotel. She was mysteriously drawn into the meeting room to hear the Bible teaching. At the end of the service, those with needs were invited to come forward for prayer. Della responded.

When Della reached the front of the room, she was approached by a lady and two men. Before they reached her, she groaned loudly and fell to the floor. The three individuals prayed for her, but did not attempt to lift her up. Della laid on the floor for several minutes. The lady who prayed for her saw a giant hand reach down inside of Della and pull from her the ugly blackness and darkness. She was healed, delivered, and freed from the oppression of the devil.

"If the Son sets you free, you shall be free indeed." *John 8:36 NKV*

TEACHING:

"...God anointed Jesus, Who went about doing good and healing all who were oppressed by the devil..." *Acts 10:38 NKJV*

The word "oppressed" is translated from the Greek word, "katadunasteuo", which means to exercise dominion against; to oppress.[8]

The oppression may initially occur through a hurtful word spoken, a physical or sexual abuse, or an addictive behavior.

If the hurt is allowed to fester within one, then Satan's agents will bring additional packages and messages to accompany the hurt: anger, discouragement, depression, rejection, rebellion, etc. and etc.

Satan's agents will continue to harass and oppress individuals, including Christians, until he/she learns to use the sword of the Spirit against them, that is, the *Word of God* in the same manner that Jesus used it.

COST OF THIS EXCHANGE:

When Jesus died on the cross, His soul had to spend three days and three nights in Hades, the place of departed souls. He gave one sign to the Scribes and Pharisees: the sign of Jonah. "As Jonah was in the whale's belly for three days and three nights, so the Son of Man will be in the heart of the Earth for three days and three nights." *Matthew 12:39-40 KJV*

Jesus was laid in the lowest pit (*Psalm 88 NKJV*). He stated, "darkness and terror are My constant companions." He was oppressed to a degree that no one else has ever been oppressed. He was surrounded by the shrieking demons of Hades.

He was taking my place and yours in Hades, in the lowest pit, and paying the cost for your deliverance and freedom from oppression.

RESPONSE:

The Scripture states that "the Lord is never discouraged." Christ is in me. Therefore, I will not be discouraged. I make a deliberate decision by an act of my will, that I will not give in to discouragement that often leads to oppression. I also decide that I will quickly forgive all those who hurt me and offend me, which will free me from those very hurts and offenses. I do this knowingly, on the basis of the cross—on the basis that Jesus took the offenses so that I would not have to carry them.

PERSONAL NOTES—CHAPTER 10

1. What is the meaning of the Greek word, *catadunasteuo*?

    _____

    _____

    _____

    _____

2. What is the assignment of Satan's agents to the Christian or unbeliever who does not respond to hurtful words or hurtful actions in a spiritual manner?

    _____

    _____

    _____

    _____

3. What was the cost for this exchange?

    _____

    _____

    _____

    _____

4. What was the result of God anointing Jesus?

    _____

    _____

    _____

    _____

EXCHANGE # 11

MY EMOTIONAL HURTS FOR HIS HEALING

THEME SCRIPTURE:

ISAIAH 61:01—"...the Lord...has sent Me to heal the brokenhearted..." *NKJV*

ILLUSTRATION:

A certain minister was praying for the sick and oppressed. After he had prayed for several, a middle-aged woman stood before him for prayer. She stated that she had carried arthritis in her shoulders for more than 15 years. The minister received a "Word of Knowledge" and immediately asked the woman, "who do you need to forgive?" The woman began to cry and replied, "my mother". She was led through the process of forgiveness and was immediately healed.

TEACHING:

Jesus took the offenses that have impacted you—those very offenses that have caused hurts, rejection, and broken hearts. This is the basis for forgiveness.

KEYS TO FORGIVENESS:

- Understand that forgiveness is a decision—not an emotion.
- Know that forgiveness is a demand from the Father.
- Understand that forgiveness is based on the cross.
- Understand that Jesus has already carried the offenses that hurt you.

MAINTAIN FORGIVENESS:

- Decide to win the battle with your mind and your emotions.
- Remind the enemy: "I made a decision to forgive. This decision will not change."
- Remind your emotions: "I made a decision to forgive. That decision will not change. Emotions, you must come into agreement with my decision."

COST OF THIS EXCHANGE:

Jesus was despised and rejected. *Isaiah 53:03 KJV* "He came unto His own and His own **received Him not.**" *John 1:11 KJV* He suffered from the offenses. His attitude even before the cross took place is illustrated as He overlooked Jerusalem. "How often I would have gathered you, even as a hen gathers her flock, but you would not." *Matthew 23:37 NKJV*

RESPONSE:

Ask the Holy Spirit to help you in making a list of all those who have hurt you and offended you. Obey the Scriptures that instruct you to forgive those who have offended you. Remind yourself that the act of forgiving is based upon the cross. That is, that Jesus took every offense that has been and will be directed at you.

Jesus said, "If you forgive others their trespasses... your Heavenly Father will also forgive you. But if you do not forgive others... then your Father will not forgive your trespasses." *Matthew 6:15 Amplified*

PERSONAL NOTES—EXCHANGE 11:

1. What are the four keys to forgiveness?

_____

_____

_____

_____

2. How does one maintain forgiveness?

_____

_____

_____

_____

3. What cost did Jesus endure so that we could forgive?

_____

_____

_____

_____

4. What should be the response of the Christian who has been hurt?

_____

_____

_____

_____

EXCHANGE # 12

MY STRESS FOR HIS PEACE

THEME SCRIPTURE: "Peace I leave with you. My peace I give to you, not as the world gives..." *John 14:27 NKJV*

Isaiah 53:05— "...The chastisement for our peace was upon Him..." *NKJV*

ILLUSTRATION:

Edward was compelled to constantly be involved in an activity. If he was not "on the move" he experienced much dissatisfaction. In spite of his many physical activities, he was seeking more. He was continually seeking acceptance by buying a bigger, more expensive house, a more stylish wardrobe, or new cars. He sought an upgrade in all things.

He openly appealed to men and women who were politically powerful in his city and state. He sought to be influential in his community. He shunned those who did not live up to his guidelines.

Edward was always stressed out concerning his job, his need to be accepted in the right circles, and his inability to measure up to the standards of the elite class of society.

Edward was continually stressed in all areas of his life.

STRESS—THE ENEMY OF PEACE:

Examples of stress include:

- Routine stress related to the pressures of school, work, family, and other daily responsibilities.
- Stress brought about by a sudden negative change, such as losing a job, divorce, or illness.
- Traumatic stress experienced during an event such as a major accident, war, assault, or natural disaster where people may be in danger of being seriously hurt or killed. People who experience traumatic stress may have very distressing temporary emotional and physical symptoms, but most recover naturally soon after.

2. **Not all stress is bad:**

In a dangerous situation, stress signals the body to prepare to face a threat or flee to safety. In these situations, your pulse quickens, you breathe faster, your muscles tense, and your brain uses more oxygen and increases activity—all functions aimed at survival and in response to stress. In non-life-threatening situations, stress can motivate people, such as when they need to take a test or interview for a new job.

3. Long-term stress can harm your health:

Coping with the impact of chronic stress can be challenging. Because the source of long-term stress is more constant than acute stress, the body never receives a clear signal to return to normal functioning. With chronic stress, those same lifesaving reactions in the body can disturb the immune, digestive, cardiovascular, sleep, and reproductive systems. Some people may experience mainly digestive symptoms, while others may have headaches, sleeplessness, sadness, anger, or irritability.

Over time, continued strain on your body from stress may contribute to serious health problems, such as heart disease, high blood pressure, diabetes, and other illnesses, including mental disorders such as depression or anxiety.[9]

TEACHING:

PEACE—A BENEFIT OF THE NEW BIRTH/NEW COVENANT:

Therefore, having been justified by faith, we have peace with God through our Lord Jesus Christ. *Romans 5:1*

THE IMPORTANCE OF SPEAKING PEACE TO YOURSELF AND OTHERS:

Paul began his letters with this greeting:

Romans 1:7— "To all who are in Rome, beloved of God, called to be saints: Grace to you and peace from God our Father and the Lord Jesus Christ." *NKJV*

I Corinthians 1:3— "Grace to you and peace from God our Father and the Lord Jesus Christ." *NKJV*

Galatians 1:3— "Grace to you and peace from God our Father and the Lord Jesus Christ." *NKJV*

PEACE THROUGH SIMPLE FAITH IN THE WORD:

Know that your security is in Jesus alone. "I will both lie down and sleep in peace. For You alone, O Lord, make me dwell in safety." *Psalms 4:08 KJV*

AN EXTRAORDINARY KIND OF PEACE:

Be anxious for nothing, but in everything by prayer and supplication, with thanksgiving, let your requests be made known to God, and the peace of God, which surpasses all understanding, will guard your hearts and minds through Christ Jesus. *Philippians 4:6-7 NKJV*

HIS PEACE IS SUPPORTED BY HIS POWER AND POSSESSED BY FAITH:

The following event was described in *Mark 4:33-41 NKJV:* The disciples were in a boat with Jesus on the Sea of Galilee. It had been a long day, filled with crowds of people. The disciples were tired. Jesus was asleep. A storm arose on the sea. It was sudden and immediately life-threatening. The disciples feared for their lives. Then they remembered that Jesus was in the boat. They cried out to Him, "Teacher, do You not care that we are perishing?" Then He arose and rebuked the wind, and said to the sea, "Peace, be still!" And the wind ceased and there was a great calm. But He said to them, "Why are you so fearful? How is it that you have no faith?"

THE COST OF THIS EXCHANGE:

Jesus experienced the total absence of peace for 3 days and 3 nights. The prophetic Psalmist declared, "You have laid me in the lowest pit. *Psalms 88:6 NKJV* Darkness and Terror are my constant companions. You will not leave my soul in Hades nor allow my body to see corruption." *Psalms 16:10 NKJV* Peter reveals to us through his sermon on the Day of Pentecost that the Psalmist was not speaking of himself, but he had been referring to the future experiences of Jesus. *Acts 2:27-31 NKJV*

RESPONSE:

Be anxious for nothing. Do not worry. *Philippians 4:06 NKJV*

Let not your heart be troubled. *John 14:01 NKJV*

Make your requests known to God with thanksgiving. *Philippians 4:06 NKJV*

Cast your stress and anxiety and worry upon Him. *I Peter 5:07 NKJV*

Receive His peace by faith—believing His promise. *Mark 4:41 NKJV*

Treat fear, worry, and stress as an enemy, attempting to enter your home. *II Corinthians 10:4-5 NKJV*

Dismiss fear, worry, and stress from your soul as messages from Satan. *II Corinthians 10:4-5 KJV*

Speak His peace to yourself. *Ephesians 5:19; Colossians 3:16 NKJV*

Sing His peace to yourself. *Psalms 105:02; James 5:13 NKJV*

PERSONAL NOTES—EXCHANGE 12

What is God's offer of exchange for our stress?

_____

_____

What type of peace does God offer?

_____

_____

List three examples which could cause stress.

_____

_____

What was the cost for this exchange?

_____

_____

List six ways to respond in achieving and maintaining this peace.

_____

_____

_____

_____

_____

_____

EXCHANGE # 13

MY BROKEN LIFE
FOR HIS BEAUTY

THEME SCRIPTURE:

ISAIAH 61:1-3— "The Spirit of the Lord God is upon Me, for He has anointed Me to give beauty for ashes..." *NKJV*

ILLUSTRATION:

Dillon was a young, hard-working man from the Northwest region of the US. He had met a beautiful young woman and fallen in love with her. They had been married for only a year and 6 months, when he detected a change. Upon returning from a business trip, he discovered his wife entertaining another man in their home. He was devastated—deeply hurt.

After his divorce, he wandered into a church one Sunday morning. He heard singing and anointed teaching. It stirred a heart that had been broken. He was drawn to the love that the people in that church exhibited.

Over a period of three months, he was continually touched by the moving of the Holy Spirit in his life. He began to build his life again from the spiritual truths that he was quickly learning. He awakened one morning to discover that he no longer was hurting. He was amazed at the love and the power of God to heal his broken life.

SPIRITUAL MAKEOVER:

"The Potter saw a vessel that was broken by the wind and the rain.

And He sought with so much compassion to make it over anew.

And I was that vessel...then God picked up the pieces of my broken life that day.

And He made me a new vessel..."[10] Andre Crouch

Paul used the example of the Potter and the Clay in *Romans 9:19-24 NKJV*, to explain that God is the Creator and has formed us in a distinct manner. Yet, there are many who complain about the way they look or the abilities that they lack. God has assignments for Christians. Once an individual discovers that assignment, God then gives the individual spiritual gifts and abilities, in order to help the individual to complete his/her assignment.

In our counseling over the years, we have often encountered those who had high goals for their lives, but rejected their goals and dreams when disappointments came, or when relationships were broken. God specializes in makeovers, that is, He can remold, remake, and repair those broken vessels, thereby fashioning the "ashes into beauty".

THE COST OF THIS EXCHANGE:

Jesus was despised and rejected. He was abused. Angry soldiers spit in His face. His back was scarred with multiple beatings. A crown of thorns was thrust upon His head. Then He was nailed to the cross.

In addition, while He hung on the cross, God placed all of your hurts and abuses upon Him. He had to carry the hurts, rejections, and abuses of the entire world. Why? Because God wanted you to be free of the hurts, rejections, and abuses. You were never meant to carry them. You were never meant to hold on to them.

RESPONSE:

Allow the Lord to remove the scars from your mind and your emotions. Your soul will try to hang on to the hurts and the memories of the abuses. Give them up. Give them all to Jesus. Let Him remake you—even as the Potter remakes the broken vessel.

Forgive those who have offended you and hurt you. Get rid of the ashes—the scars—the memories of abuses. Bring your broken vessel to the Lord. He specializes in spiritual makeovers.

"Lord, I come to You as a broken person—with broken dreams—broken relationships. I trust you to make me over anew. Give me a new beginning. Take my scars—remove the hurts—as I forgive those who have hurt me. In Jesus Name, Amen."

PERSONAL NOTES—EXCHANGE 13

What is the exchange offered in Isaiah 61:03 NKJV?

_____

_____

What is the example feature in Andre Crouch's song?

_____

_____

What was the cost for this exchange?

_____

_____

_____

_____

What should be the response to this offer of exchange?

_____

_____

_____

_____

_____

EXCHANGE # 14

MY LACK FOR HIS SUFFICIENCY

THEME SCRIPTURE:

II Corinthians 9:08— "God is able to make all grace abound to you, so that you, having all sufficiency in all things at all times, may abound to all good works." *NKJV*

MY LACK FOR HIS ABUNDANCE:

- Every spiritual benefit and blessing is by grace through faith. "For by grace you are saved *(SOZO*—Greek word) through faith, and even that is a gift from God." *Ephesians 2:08 NKJV*
- *Sozo* is translated saved or salvation in the English. It encompasses every spiritual blessing and every spiritual experience in God.
- This specific benefit (abundance) is also provided by God's grace through faith.

PAUL'S EXHORTATION—*II CORINTHIANS 9:*

II CORINTHIANS 9:08: "And God is able to make all grace abound toward you, so that you, always having all sufficiency in all things, may abound to all good works." *KJV*

GRACE=God's enabling power. Grace enables the believer to do what otherwise he/she could not do. In this case, grace enables the believer to give abundantly to the work of the Lord. Grace enables the believer to be what otherwise he/she could not be. In this case, grace enables the believer to be a GIVER. Grace enables the believer to receive what otherwise he/she could not receive. In this case, grace enables the believer to receive the abundant return of financial blessing from the Lord.

Please note the number of times that abundance is inferred in the above verse:

- **ALL** GRACE OR EVERY GRACE
- MAKE GRACE **ABOUND** TO YOU
- ALWAYS—AT **ALL** TIMES
- **ALL** SUFFICIENCY
- IN **ALL** THINGS
- MAY **ABOUND** TO **ALL** GOOD WORKS.

I repeat the above phrase: "...so that you.... may abound to all good works." *II Corinthians 9:08 KJV* This must be the end goal for every believer who expects great financial blessings from the Lord. God is saying to us, "I'm causing my grace to abound to you so that you may abound to good works. I'm supplying to you all sufficiency, in all things, at all times, so that you may abound to all good works."

It is logical to assume that a believer who has an abundance of money would be able to do more for the Lord than a believer who has a lack of money. There have been times when I learned of a friend in need, and I had nothing to give to him. I learned of friends who needed encouragement or the prayer of faith for healing and I could not go to them because they were thousands of miles away and I had not the available funds to travel. I could have done so much more if I only had possessed sufficiency of funds.

ILLUSTRATION:

An individual might need gasoline for his/her vehicle. He/she drives to the nearest gas station, needing to fill the tank in order to take a trip. He/she needs $45 in order to fill the tank with gasoline. He/she checks his/her funds. To his/her chagrin, he/she only has $20.

That is a lack of sufficiency.

If the individual has $100—that is more than enough—that is sufficiency.

If the individual has 1000s of dollars set aside for the trip—that is an abundance.

Sufficiency— (Greek word=autarkeia)—Strong's # 841.[11]

Sufficiency—definition=more than enough. Enough so that one can "abound to all (every) good work."

The purpose of the sufficiency or the abundance is to equip the believer so that he/she can give generously to all good works. In many cases, the "good works" will not take place unless someone gives an offering. The subject of *II Corinthians, chapter 9*, is giving.

Bill Patterson and his wife Vicki often sing the chorus, He's more than enough:

"He's more than enough—more than enough.

He is El Shaddai—the God of Plenty—

The All-Sufficient One—God Almighty—

He is more than enough."12 [*Author—David Ingles*]

SUFFICIENCY IN ALL THINGS:

I have written concerning the lack of money simply because it is easily understood. However, Jesus took care of every lack: lack of spiritual power, lack of faith, lack of grace, lack of money. He supplied, through the grace of God, an abundance—a sufficiency in all things at all times—so that we would always be equipped to have an abundance of good works.

COST OF THIS EXCHANGE:

When Jesus was on the cross, He lacked in all things. He was hungry. He had not eaten for 24 hours. He was thirsty. He had no water to drink. He was naked. His clothing had been stripped from Him. This was the price that Jesus paid in order for us to enjoy His abundance.

RESPONSE:

The gospel means *good news*. This exchange is one of many that seems too good to be true. But it cost Jesus all that He had as He hung on the cross. Therefore, I do not have the right as a believer to reject this exchange.

PRAYER OF ACCEPTANCE:

"I gladly and joyfully accept your gift of abundance in every area of my life, so that I may abound in the end goal of this exchange: the abundance of good works.

Father, I thank you for your provision through your son, Jesus. I accept and embrace your grace that provides for me your abundance. It supplies sufficiency in all things at all times. Therefore, I am enabled to abound in every good work—in the name of Jesus, Amen."

PERSONAL NOTES—EXCHANGE 14

What is the title of the EXCHANGE that is featured in this chapter?

_____

_____

By what process does abundance come?

_____

_____

_____

List the examples of abundance that is inferred in _II Corinthians 9:08_ NKJV.

_____

_____

_____

_____

_____

_____

_____

What is the end goal of "all sufficiency"?

_____

_____

_____

What was the cost for this EXCHANGE?

_____

_____

_____

_____

List five areas of lack that are covered in this EXCHANGE.

_____

_____

_____

_____

EXCHANGE # 15

MY FEAR FOR A HEALTHY MIND

THEME SCRIPTURE:

II Tim 1:07—"God has not given us a spirit of fear, but love, power, and a sound mind." *NKJV*

ILLUSTRATION:

When my granddaughter was three, she began experiencing severe seizures. Fear came in the same "package" with the seizures. Even after the seizures ceased to occur, Emmaus would wake up in the night in the grip of fear.

My daughter-in-law created a three by five booklet with illustrations that demonstrated the promises of God concerning fear. Emmaus could not yet read; however, she was taught the promise of God that was illustrated by a picture in the booklet. If she was awakened by the fear, she would simply reach for the booklet, turn to a certain page, and quote the promise, "God has not given us a spirit of fear, but of love and power and a healthy mind." In her mind, the promise from God became stronger than the spirit of fear, thus instilling peace in her mind and heart.

TEACHING:

Contrast fear and faith:

Fear is an evil spirit—a thief to rob you of your faith. Satan has agents of fear. They are assigned to us in order to keep us from our destiny in God. Fear can keep you from your assignment in God. Fear can limit you from knowing yourself—the "real you".

ACTIONS OF FAITH:

Cast out fear; "And these signs will follow those who believe: they shall cast out (expel) demons…" *Mark 16:17 KJV* You, as a believer, can command the spirit of fear to leave you. Dismiss that spirit from yourself—dismiss his assignment against you. If fear persists in your life, submit yourself to a minister who is a believer, so that you can be freed from fear.

Study God's word:

The Gospel is the power of God unto deliverance. By hearing and/or studying the Word of God, you can expect to be delivered from the bad habits that control parts of your life.

Know your identity and your benefits:

- As a Christian, I am a new creation, a brand-new person— old things (like fear) are passed away—all things are new—all things are of God. *II Corinthians 5:17 NKJV*
- I am the righteousness of God in Christ. *II Corinthians 5:21 NKJV*
- I have been redeemed from the hand of the enemy. *Psalms 107:02 NKJV*
- The Lord is my strength and my defense. *Psalms 118:14 NKJV*
- The Lord is my refuge and my fortress—I will trust in Him; *Psalms 91:02 NKJV*
- The Lord is my light and my salvation. Of whom shall I be afraid? *Psalms 27:01 NKJV*
- Greater is He that is in me than he that is in the world. *I John 4:04 NKJV*

COST OF THIS EXCHANGE:

Jesus declared from His place in the lowest pit of Hades: "…terrors have cut me off. My acquaintances are far from me." *Psalms 88:8;16 NKJV* Hades was the territory of Satan and his demons. Satan's agent, Terror, was actively harassing Jesus for three days and three nights—in His face!

Another part of the cost that Jesus paid was His triumph over Satan and his agents. When Jesus had fulfilled every part of the sacrifice that was required to restore Adamic mankind to the intended place on the Earth, God justified Him—made Him righteous!

Jesus then disarmed Satan and his principalities and powers, and triumphed over them, making a public spectacle of them for all of Heaven to see. *Colossians 2:15 NKJV*

Because of this price that Jesus paid, He offers to us love, power, and a sound mind. Once again, we get the *best of the trade.*

RESPONSE:

The Lord is my Light and my Salvation, of whom shall I be afraid? *Psalms 27:1-2 NKJV* Greater is He that is in me than he that is in the world. *I John 4:04 NKJV* This Scriptural declaration is the motivation for living free of fear.

I will say to the Lord, "You are my refuge and my fortress."—My place of safety and protection; my fortified position, designed for both offense and defense against the enemy of fear.

If terror rises all around me, I will not fear—I will not be afraid, for You, O Lord, are my strength and my redeemer—my rock and my fortress. Instead, on the basis of your TRIUMPH, I will receive Your love, Your power, and a sound and healthy mind."

PERSONAL NOTES—EXCHANGE 15

What is the EXCHANGE that is listed in *II Timothy 1:07 NKJV*?

_____

_____

_____

_____

What is the motive of the spirit of fear?

_____

_____

_____

_____

List seven benefits that you have through your identity in Christ.

_____

_____

_____

_____

_____

_____

_____

What was the cost of this EXCHANGE?

_____

_____

_____

_____

What was the action of Jesus when God justified Him, making Him righteous?

_____

_____

_____

_____

EXCHANGE # 16

MY LONELINESS FOR HIS CONSTANT FELLOWSHIP

THEME SCRIPTURES:

"My God why have you forsaken Me?" *Matthew 27:46 NKJV*

Proverbs 24:18 NKJV "A man who has friends must himself be friendly, but there is a friend who sticks closer than a brother."

"to the praise of the glory of His grace, we are accepted in the beloved." *Ephesians 1:06 NKJV*

DEFINITION OF LONELINESS:

Loneliness is the state of distress or discomfort that results when one perceives a gap between one's desires for social connection and actual experiences of it. Even some people who are surrounded by others throughout the day—or are in a long-lasting marriage—still experience a deep and pervasive **loneliness.**[13]

ILLUSTRATION:

Susan was a freshman at a High School that was located in the Midwest. There were more than 2000 students in her High School—students of every race and culture. However, Susan was a very lonely girl.

Susan dreaded going to school every morning. She was an excellent student and seemed noticeably confident in every area of school. But inwardly, she felt completely out of place—alone.

Susan loved her church, especially the youth group. On the advice of her parents, she made an appointment to meet with her Youth Pastor. He explained to her the manner in which Jesus paid the price, so that she would not be a captive to loneliness. He prayed with her, asking that God would send the right kind of friends to her.

The Youth Pastor told her that he had been invited to speak at the Student Christian club that met on Tuesdays at her High School campus. She attended and met several students from each of the grades. Susan began to meet three or four of the students for lunch each day at school.

During the next few weeks, Susan's problem of loneliness melted away.

TEACHING:

It was a scandal when anyone was sentenced to die on a cross. The Romans, through experimentation, had created a type of execution that promised public humiliation, intense pain, and total separation from loved ones. Therefore, we should not be surprised that the disciples forsook Him. We should not be surprised that some of the people thought that He had done something terribly wrong for God to punish Him to this extent.

Jesus had been rejected by the people that He came to save. When given the choice to save Him or one of the thieves, the people cried, "crucify Him". Peter, being one of the closest disciples to Jesus, stated that He had never known this Jesus. The other disciples were scattered, confused, hopeless.

However, the Holy Spirit rolls back the curtain of revelation to reveal that Jesus was dealing with the power of sin. He was dealing with sickness, oppression, and loneliness.

COST OF THIS EXCHANGE:

While Jesus was on the cross, "God made Him to be SIN (sin nature), so that we could be the righteousness of God in Christ." *II Corinthians 5:21 NKJV* This action immediately curtailed the union that Jesus had with His Father God. God turned His back (so to speak) on His Son, cutting off the fellowship that they had enjoyed.

From this moment on, Jesus had to carry out the details of His sacrifice alone. He had stated that, "I and the Father are one." *John 10:30; John 14:10 NKJV* He had given up everything, and in this moment, He gave up union and fellowship with His Father. He did this, so that His rich fellowship could be extended to you.

RESPONSE:

- By faith in the Word, exchange loneliness and the threat of loneliness for His fellowship and the fellowship with God's people.
- Remind yourself that Scripture promised that He would be closer than a brother. *Proverbs 24:19 NKJV*
- Remind yourself that Jesus said, "I will never leave you nor forsake you."

Hebrews 13:05 NKJV

- Surround yourself by spiritually minded people.
- Through prayer, establish close fellowship with spiritually mature friends.
- Thank the Lord for submitting to the deepest of loneliness, so that He could reach you and minister to you in your loneliness.

PERSONAL NOTES—EXCHANGE 16:

What is the title of the EXCHANGE listed in this chapter?

_____

_____

What is the definition of loneliness?

_____

_____

_____

_____

What happened to Jesus when God made Him to be SIN (sin-nature)?

_____

_____

_____

_____

What are the five actions that one who is lonely should take?

_____

_____

_____

_____

_____

_____

What was the cost for this EXCHANGE?

_____

_____

_____

_____

EXCHANGE # 17

MY CONFORMITY TO THIS WORLD FOR HIS TRANSFORMATION

THEME SCRIPTURE:

Romans 12:1-2— "Be not conformed to this world, but be transformed by the renewing of your mind..." *KJV*

ILLUSTRATION:

Jim had been a committed Christian for twenty-five years. There had always been a hunger in him spiritually, like something was missing. He attended a summer seminar in the Rocky Mountains and heard a teaching on Spirit, Soul, and Body. He learned that when he first came to God through Jesus, that his born again experience actually took place in his spirit. Although, his spirit had been made alive, born again, he learned that his soul had not been born again. He heard for the first time, that his soul had to be transformed. *Romans 12:02 KJV* Also, to his surprise, he learned that it was up to him alone to ensure that the transformation would take place. Jim himself would be responsible to take his mind, will, and emotions through a systematic study of the Word of God. He made the commitment that summer to make sure that his soul would continually be transformed.

TEACHING:

SOUL—MIND, WILL, EMOTIONS:

Psuche is the Greek word for *soul.*

Psuche— (Greek word)-*Strong's #5590*, meaning mind, will, and emotions.[14]

Whereas the spirit of man must be born again, the soul of man must be transformed— radically changed. To accomplish this, the mind must be renewed, the will must conform to the will of God, and the emotions must be retrained.

MIND:

Romans 12:02 NKJV— "Do not be conformed to this world, but be transformed by the renewing of your mind, so that you may be able to prove the good, the acceptable, and the perfect will of God."

YOU DON'T THINK LIKE GOD THINKS:

God said, "My thoughts are not your thoughts nor are your ways my ways. For as the heavens are higher than the earth, so are My ways higher than your ways, and My thoughts than your thoughts." *Isaiah 55:8-9*

God is saying, "You don't think like I think. Our thoughts are incompatible. You need to change the way that you think. In order to change your thinking, you must submit your mind to My Word."

THE MIND IS A BATTLEFIELD:

The mind has been called by many Bible teachers a battlefield. *II Corinthians 10:3-5 NKJV* "For though we walk in the flesh, we do not war according to the flesh. For the weapons of our warfare are not carnal (earthly), but mighty in God:"

- Pulling down strongholds (of the enemy).
- Casting down imaginations.
- Casting down reasonings.
- Bringing every thought captive to the obedience of Christ.

Thoughts, reasonings, and imaginations are produced by the mind. This is the area where most of the battles with the enemy of believers take place.

THE MIGHTY WEAPONS ARE:

- **The Word of God**; God's Word is powerful and alive, teaching men/women how to live.
- **The Name of Jesus**; The Name of Jesus is higher than any other name.
- **The Blood of Jesus**—The Eternal offering for sins and the sin nature.

The mighty spiritual weapons are the only weapons available that deal effectively with imaginations, reasonings, wrong thoughts, fears, depression, and every strategy that the enemy brings against individuals.

The weapons are activated by:

- **Prayer:** Believers pray in the Name of Jesus; believers pray using promises found in the Word.
- **Praise:** Believers praise the Name of Jesus, which drives the enemy away.
- **Teaching:** Pastors and teachers teach the Word of God, equipping believers to have victory over the enemy.
- **Confession or testimony**—Believers confess what the Word promises to them; believers confess what the Word declares that the Blood of Jesus has done for them.

Please note that the mouth or the voice is used to activate each of the weapons for use against the enemy.

EMOTIONS:

The experience of the new birth does not save or sanctify the mind or the emotions. The emotions, as with the thought life, must be submitted to the process of sanctification, that is, speaking the Word of God to the thoughts and emotions of one's soul. The emotions have been accustomed to "going their own way", and must be retrained, reigned in. The relationships and Christian service of the Christian are too important to be determined by the emotions.

THE WILL:

The Bible gives us the example of Jesus as He prayed in the garden just before His arrest, trial, and crucifixion. He prayed, "…if it be possible, let this cup pass from me, nevertheless, not my will but your will be done." *Luke 22:42 NKJV*

Knowing full well exactly what He was facing, Jesus went through the difficulty of conforming His will to the will of the Father.

Christians will have many opportunities in their life and service to the Lord to do the same, that is, to conform to the will of God.

COST OF THIS BENEFIT:

Jesus said: "Lo, I have come to do your will. I find your will in the volume of the book. (Word of God)." *Hebrews 10:7-10 NKJV* This statement reveals to us that Jesus had submitted both His mind and His will to the Word of God.

RESPONSE:

Make a decision: "I will win the battle of the mind & the soul with the help of the Holy Spirit.

In obedience to the Word in Romans 12:02 *KJV* I commit to renew my mind through a systematic study of the Word of God. By this action, I will no longer conform to the thinking and actions of the world.

PERSONAL NOTES—EXCHANGE 17

What is the EXCHANGE that is featured in this chapter?

_____

_____

What is the activity that a Christian must perform in order to be transformed?

_____

_____

_____

_____

What happens in the three areas of the soul as it is transformed?

_____

_____

_____

_____

List the four results that occur when a Christian's mighty spiritual weapons are activated?

_____

_____

_____

_____

List the three major spiritual weapons.

_____

_____

_____

_____

How are the spiritual weapons activated?

_____

_____

_____

_____

What is a reasonable response to this EXCHANGE?

_____

_____

_____

_____

EXCHANGE # 18

MY POVERTY FOR HIS RICHES

THEME SCRIPTURE:

II Corinthians 8:09— "You know the grace of our Lord, in that, though He was rich, for our sakes He became poor, so that we, through His poverty, might be rich." *NKJV*

ILLUSTRATION:

Harry grew up in a small town in the Midwest. He had four siblings, an alcoholic father, and a loving mother. This region had depended mainly on minerals mined from the ground. The minerals were no longer a necessity in the US economy. Therefore, the local economy began to suffer. Most families were poor, but somehow survived with little income.

Harry developed a mindset of poverty. Nothing he did seemed to work for him and his family. His expectations were extremely low. After several years with this attitude, Harry was invited to a seminar by a friend. He reluctantly attended the seminar and was intrigued by the Bible instruction that he received on finances and giving. He had believed that he was too poor to give anything to his church, not even an offering.

The instruction on giving to the Lord transformed the mind of Harry. He made a commitment at the end of the seminar to become a giver to the Kingdom of God. Over the next few years, Harry advanced from the poverty class to the middle class of income earners. Eventually, Harry would start his own business and would begin to prosper. He claims now that he gave his way out of poverty.

There are countless stories in America just like the story of Harry.

TEACHING:

When Jesus began His ministry, He read an account from *Isaiah 61: NKJV* "The Spirit of the Lord God is upon Me, for the Lord has anointed Me to preach good tidings (good news) to the poor...."

Poverty is listed in Deuteronomy 28 as a curse. Notice *verse 47* of *Deuteronomy 28*: "Because you did not serve the Lord your God with joy and gladness of heart, **<u>for the abundance of everything,</u>** (48) therefore you shall serve your enemies, whom the Lord will send against you, in hunger, in thirst, in nakedness, and in the need of everything...." *NKJV*

Component parts of poverty: HUNGER; THIRST; NAKEDNESS; THE LACK OF EVERYTHING.

What would be good news to the poor? You do not have to be poor anymore. We are aware of this good news because of the price that Jesus paid, specifically to the poor. Jesus not only preached good news to the poor, He also identified with them. He became poor when He was on the cross. He was rich when He was on the Earth as a human. However, as He hung upon the cross, He was hungry; He was thirsty; He was naked; He had lost everything—even His robe and clothing were taken away from Him. He had nothing left.

Spiritually, He also became poor. Because of God's perfect plan, Jesus identified with us in our needs. When God made Him to be sin, *(II Corinthians 5:21 KJV)*, the following changes occurred in the spiritual life of Jesus:

His spirit became dead to God because of sin.

His nature was changed from righteousness to sin nature.

His union with the Father was cut off.

He no longer had fellowship with His father.

From the moment that He became sin, He suffered completely alone. He uttered, "My God, why have You forsaken Me?" *Mark 14:34 NKJV*

His loneliness continued after His body gave up its breath and life. His body was placed in the tomb (sepulcher), but His soul went to Hades. Peter reveals this truth to us in his sermon on the day of Pentecost, when He quoted from *Psalms 16:8-11 NKJV*: "You will not leave My soul in Hades, nor will You allow Your Holy One to see corruption." Peter explains to the Jews on the Day of Pentecost that David was not speaking of himself, but was prophesying of the death and resurrection of Jesus (*Acts 2:25-32 NKJV*). Jesus cried out from Hades, as prophesied by David: (*Psalms 88; Psalms 16:10 NKJV*) "You have laid Me in the lowest Pit-in the darkest place. Terror surrounds Me like a flood. My closest companion is darkness. Will there be a resurrection in the morning?" (read entire chapter)

Jesus had given a sign to the Scribes: "As Jonah was in the belly of the whale for three days and three nights, so the Son of Man will be in the heart of the Earth for three days and three nights." *Matthew 12:40 NKJV* The above verse (Psalms 88: Psalms 16:10 *NKJV*) places Jesus in the lowest pit. As in every area of human need, Jesus had to go to the very bottom—to experience the worst of every human need.

In this manner, Jesus experienced physical poverty and also spiritual poverty. He did so, in order to offer us the following exchange: "For you know the grace of our Lord Jesus Christ, in that, though He was rich, for our sakes, He became poor, so that we, through His poverty, might be rich." *II Corinthians 08:09 NKJV*

COST OF THIS EXCHANGE:

Jesus experienced the Scriptural definition of poverty during His sacrifice on the cross. He declared, "I thirst". He was hungry. He had not eaten for twenty-four hours. He was naked on the cross. He had nothing. Everything had been taken from Him. Deuteronomy 28:46-48—"Because you did not serve the Lord your God with joy and gladness of heart, **for the abundance of everything,** (48) therefore you shall serve your enemies, whom the Lord will send against you, in hunger, in thirst, in nakedness, and in the need of everything." *NKJV*

He became poor for my sake; He became hungry for my sake; He became naked on the cross for my sake; He was thirsty for my sake; He lacked in all areas of life for my sake.

RESPONSE:

"Thank You, Lord, for submitting Yourself to extreme poverty, so that I could enjoy riches, both in this life and the life to come.

PERSONAL NOTES—EXCHANGE 18

Write the verse from II Corinthians 8:09, NKJV.

_____

_____

_____

_____

What is the reason listed in _Deuteronomy, chapter 28, NKJV_, which led God's people into poverty?

_____

_____

_____

_____

List the four component parts of poverty.

_____

_____

_____

_____

Explain the revelation that Peter gave in his Pentecostal message concerning the soul of Jesus.

_____

_____

_____

_____

What was the only sign that Jesus gave to the Scribes?

_____

_____

_____

_____

List the four ways in which Jesus suffered poverty.

_____

_____

_____

_____

EXCHANGE # 19

MY SENTENCE TO HADES FOR THE PROMISE OF HEAVEN

THEME SCRIPTURE:

Acts 2:27 NKJV— "For You will not leave My soul in Hades, nor will You allow Your Holy One to see corruption."

DEFINITIONS:

Hades is a Greek word meaning the *place of departed souls.*₁₃ Satan's keeper of Hades was also named Hades. Therefore, Hades is both a place and a Satanic being.₁₅

Gahenna is a Greek word meaning *Hell Fire* or the *Lake of Fire.*₁₆

Jesus referred to both of these terms.

Please note: Death and Hades are partners. They ride together. In the tribulation period, when the Seals of Judgment are opened, John declared, "So I looked, and behold, a pale horse. And the name of him who sat on it was Death, and Hades followed with him. And power was given to them over a fourth of the earth, to kill with sword, with hunger, with death, and by the beasts of the earth. *Revelations 4:08 KJV* In *I Corinthians, chapter 15 NKJV,* the redeemed declare victory over Death and Hades: "O Death, where is your sting? O Hades, where is your victory?" In *Revelations, chapter 20, verse 14*, "and Death and Hades were cast into the Lake of Fire. This is the second death."₁₇ *Young's Literal Translation* The last of the enemies of God's people.

ILLUSTRATION:

Lazarus and the Rich Man:

"And it came to pass, that the beggar died, and was carried by the angels into Abraham's bosom: the rich man also died, and was buried; And in Hades he lifted up his eyes, being in torment, and sees Abraham afar off, and Lazarus in his bosom. And he cried and said, Father Abraham, have mercy on me, and send Lazarus, that he may dip the tip of his finger in water, and cool my tongue; for I am tormented in this flame. But Abraham said, Son, remember that you in your lifetime received good things, and likewise Lazarus evil things: but now he is comforted, and you are tormented. And besides all this, between us and you there is a great gulf fixed: so that they which would pass from here to you cannot; neither can they pass to us, that would come from there." *Luke 16:22-26 NKJV*

TEACHING:

- When He died on the cross, the body of Jesus was placed in the tomb and His soul went to Hades—the place of the dead.
- "Sheol" is the Hebrew word in the Old Testament for the place of the dead.
- "Hades" is the Greek word in the New Testament for the place of the dead.
- Definition from Strong's Exhaustive Concordance for the words Sheol and Hades: "the place for departed souls."
- Jacob had believed the reports from his sons that Joseph had been killed by wild animals. In his old age, he stated that he would soon join his son Joseph in Sheol, and would visit with him there.
- Jesus gave His disciples this sign: "For as Jonah was three days and three nights in the belly of the great fish, so will the son of man be three days and three nights in the heart of the Earth." *Matthew 12:39-40 NKJV*
- "Now this: 'He ascended'—what does it mean, but that He also first descended into the lower parts of the Earth?" *Ephesians 4:10 KJV*
- Contrast: Christians who believe in "soul sleep" when they die and those who believe that they are "immediately in the presence of God". Those who believe in "soul sleep" tend to have a great fear of death.
- *Ps 107:26 NKJV*—they go down again to the depths.
- *Ps 130:1 NKJV*—Out of the depths have I cried unto You.
- *Prov 9:18 NKJV*—her guests are in the depths of Sheol.

Healing from physical death:

Jesus changed physical death for the Christian by going to Hades. He died alone. His body was placed in a tomb, but His soul went to Hades, the place of the dead. Peter, in his sermon on the Day of Pentecost, revealed to us that the prophetic Psalmist was speaking of Jesus, "Who would cry out from Hades, because 'You will not leave my soul in Hades, neither will You allow Your Holy One to see corruption'." *Acts 2:27 NKJV*

ADDITIONAL PROPHECIES FROM THE PSALMIST:

"You have laid Me in the lowest pit. Terror surrounds me. Darkness is my closest companion... Will there be a resurrection in the morning?" *Psalms 88 NIV Psalms 16:10 NKJV*

SIGN OF JONAH:

Jesus had given the sign of Jonah, "For as Jonah was three days and three nights in the belly of the great fish, so will the Son of Man be three days and three nights in the heart of the earth." *Matthew 12:40 NKJV* This verse indicates that Hades, the place of the dead, was in the heart (core) of the earth. "Therefore, He says: 'When He ascended on high, He led captivity captive, and gave gifts to men.' Now this, 'He ascended'—what does it mean but that He also first descended into the lower parts of the earth? He who descended is also the One who ascended far above all the heavens, that He might fulfill all things." *Ephesians 4:8-10 NKJV*

COST OF THIS EXCHANGE:

When Jesus died on the cross, His body was placed in a sepulcher. His soul went to Hades. By going to Hades, He took our place. He changed the destiny of every Christian who would die. Because He went to Hades, we do not go there. When Christians die, their spirits and souls immediately go to Heaven. Paul revealed, " therefore we will to be absent from the body, and to be present with the Lord." *I Corinthians 5:08 NKJV*

RESPONSE:

Thank You, Lord Jesus, for coming and making a New Covenant, which included making all things "new". Thank You for changing death for the Christian, whereby we are immediately in the presence of the Lord.

However, if I am still alive and remain when the Rapture takes place, I declare that I will hear the shout of the Lord, saying, "come up here". I will rise together with the resurrected saints to meet the Lord in the air. *I Thessalonians 4:13-18 NKJV*

PERSONAL NOTES—EXCHANGE 19:

List the Exchange in this chapter.

_____

_____

_____

_____

What is the meaning of the Greek word, *Hades*?

_____

_____

_____

_____

What is the meaning of the Greek word, *Gehenna*?

_____

_____

_____

_____

Who is the partner of *Hades*?

_____

_____

_____

_____

What is the clue that reveals the location of *Hades*?

_____

_____

_____

_____

What is the cost of this Exchange?

_____

_____

_____

_____

EXCHANGE # 20

MY REJECTION FOR HIS ACCEPTANCE

THEME SCRIPTURES:

Ephesians 1:06—"to the praise of His grace, by which He made us accepted in the Beloved." *NKJV*

"He was despised and rejected of men, a man of sorrows..." "He came unto His own and His own did not receive Him." *Isaiah 53:3 KJV; John 1:11 NKJV*

"My God, why have You forsaken Me?" *Matthew 27:46 NKJV*

- In the same manner that He took our sins and sicknesses, Jesus took our fears and rejections, so that we could be accepted by the Father.

ILLUSTRATION:

Stephanie was the daughter of an abusive father and a mother who was addicted to drugs. By the age of seven, she had been abused physically and sexually. She was removed from her home and placed in foster care. Therefore, the rejection syndrome began early in her life.

At the age of nine, she was adopted by a Christian couple who provided her with a safe and loving home. She appreciated the love in her new home. However, she continued to battle with the memories and scars of her previous life.

At the age of fifteen, Stephanie attended a Youth Seminar, along with some of the youth from her church. One day, the theme of the seminar was "The Answer to Rejection." She responded to the teaching and went forward for prayer at the end of the evening service.

When a counselor led her through a prayer of forgiveness for her biological parents who had abused her, all of the fear, resentment, anger, and rebellion left. She was free of all the baggage that she had carried for most of her life.

TEACHING:

REJECTION SYNDROME:

Christian counselors are working overtime, attempting to take care of all of the Christians who are suffering from rejection. It is the strategy that is most used by Satan. Why do you think that is the case? Because it has worked so well for him and is still working well for him. If Satan cannot keep an individual from accepting Christ as

Savior, then his goal becomes to keep that individual from becoming what God intended for him/her to become.

(The following lists are from my personal notes, taken during a seminar by Christian Counselors in Houston, TX in 1983.)[18]

THE MOST COMMON CAUSES FOR REJECTION:

- Abuse—mental—physical—sexual
- Mistreatment by peers
- Abandonment through adoption, divorce, or death
- Lack of self-acceptance
- Generational Curse

WRONG RESPONSES TO REJECTION:

- Hurt
- Anger
- Fear
- Insecurity
- Wrong Thoughts
- Discouragement
- Depression
- Rebellion

WRONG ADJUSTMENTS:

- Seek acceptance in wrong ways
- Fantasize—vain imaginations
- Perfectionism—if I do everything perfectly, I will not be rejected.
- Workaholic
- Focus on material things.

CONSEQUENCES OF WRONG ADJUSTMENTS:

- Inferiority complex
- Loss of identity
- Wrong treatment from peers
- Suicidal thoughts[19]

COST OF THIS EXCHANGE:

Jesus was despised and rejected of men, forsaken by His Father God, forsaken by His disciples, charged by religious leaders, and crucified by the Roman Empire. He went to the very bottom of rejection, so that no one suffering from rejection would ever be beyond His reach.

RESPONSE:

1. **CLASSIFY THE WRONG REACTIONS AND WRONG READJUSTMENTS AS SINS.**

Any thing, any person, any relationship, any emotion or feeling that keeps you from being who God intended for you to be, or keeps you from doing what God has called you to do, or keeps you from living as God intended for you to live, is SIN.

2. **CONFESS THE SIN—CALL IT BY NAME:**

Rejection—Hurt—Fear—Fear of failure—Depression—Etc.

Thank God for the forgiveness and the cleansing that you have received according to His promise in *I John 1:9 KJV*— "If we confess our sins, He is faithful and just to forgive us our sins and to cleanse us from all unrighteousness."

3. FORGIVE ALL THOSE WHO HAVE HURT YOU OR WRONGED YOU:

Ask the Holy Spirit to help you remember those who have hurt you or wronged you. Make a list. For each individual on your "hurts" list, pray a prayer of forgiveness.

Forgiveness is a decision. It is NOT an emotion. Do not let your emotions rob you of this decision. Your decision is a powerful force. Your decision is a deliberate act of your will. This decision to forgive each individual is based on the cross—on the fact that Jesus took every hurt and every offense ever committed against you by others. He did this so that you would not have to carry that load. He has already carried them, so that you would not have to carry them. Please understand that you will need to remind your emotions of your decision to forgive. This reminder will need to continue until your emotions come into line with your decision.

PRAYER OF FORGIVENESS:

Insert the name of the person that you are forgiving:

Father, I forgive__(name)_____on the basis of the cross. I forgive him/her on the basis that Jesus took this hurt so that I would not have to carry it. I forgive_(name)_____ now by a deliberate act of my will in the Name of Jesus. Amen.

KNOW THIS:

When you came to God through Jesus, He did not merely tolerate you—He welcomed you—He accepted you into His family. Thanks be to God! You are accepted!

PERSONAL NOTES—CHAPTER 20:

Write the exchange that is listed in this chapter.

_____

_____

What is the strategy that Satan most often uses in his attacks on Christians?

_____

_____

_____

_____

List the five most common causes for Rejection.

_____

_____

_____

_____

_____

_____

_____

List seven of the wrong responses to Rejection.

_____

_____

_____

_____

_____

_____

List the five wrong readjustments.

_____

_____

_____

_____

_____

List four of the consequences from wrong readjustments.

_____

_____

_____

_____

What are the three necessary responses in order to recover from hurt and Rejection?

_____

_____

_____

_____

What was the cost for this exchange?

_____

_____

EXCHANGE # 21

MY GRIEF FOR HIS OIL OF JOY

SCRIPTURE:

ISAIAH 61:1-3 KJV—"The Spirit of the Lord God is upon Me, for He has anointed me...to give the oil of joy for mourning..."

ILLUSTRATION:

Jessica received a phone call from a police officer that her daughter had been in a traffic accident and was severely injured. She and her husband raced to the hospital, where the injured passengers were taken. She prayed as they ran through the corridors of the hospital. She identified herself to a nurse of duty and asked where her daughter had been taken. Her daughter was in surgery. A doctor would be out to visit with her and her husband as soon as possible. She walked the floor in the waiting room and prayed for her daughter. Three hours later, the surgeon emerged and grimly explained that he had done all that he could. The injuries were too severe for her daughter to live.

Jessica was devastated. She walked through the affairs that were necessary for the next few days—funeral arrangements, personal effects from the wrecked car and the hospital, the thank-you cards for the grieving friends.

Then she retreated within herself and mourned. The grief was overwhelming. The grief actually paralyzed her. She could not function. She could not carry out the daily chores needed to care for her husband and her two children. She could not even show them the love that she needed to show. She became a prisoner of grief.

For three months, she stumbled through life. She told herself that she could recover and continue to love her husband, take care of her kids, and be a good church member. However, there was no longer any meaning to every-day life.

One afternoon, while walking through the park, she cried out to God. It was a desperate cry: "O Lord, this is too much for me. I cannot bear it. Please help me."

That night Jessica was awakened by a dream. She had seen her daughter in Heaven, sitting at the feet of Jesus. She appeared to be delightfully happy. She was completely safe—secure in the presence of Jesus.

The grief left—replaced by a joy of knowing her child was happy and secure.

Jessica mourned from time to time, but not like others who have grieved, but who had no hope or promise of Heaven.

TEACHING:

Grief is a natural response to loss. It's the emotional suffering you feel when something or someone you love is taken away. Often, the pain of loss can feel overwhelming. You may experience all kinds of difficult and unexpected emotions: from shock or anger to disbelief, guilt, and profound sadness. The pain of grief can also disrupt your physical health, making it difficult to sleep, eat, or even think straight. These are normal reactions to loss—and the more significant the loss, the more intense your grief will be.[19]

The good news is that there is a spiritual application—a God-ordained prescription to alleviate the pain and suffering caused by grief.

Jesus declared that He was anointed, not only to heal the sick and deliver those who were demonized, but also to give the oil of joy to those who were experiencing grief. He paid the price so that He could touch and heal those who were prisoners of grief.

God never intended for you to bear the burden of grief. Your soul was not equipped to handle that heavy load. GIVE IT TO THE LORD.

COMFORT IN THE SCRIPTURES:

"But I do not want you to be ignorant, brethren, concerning those who have fallen asleep, lest you sorrow as others who have no hope." *I Thessalonians 4:13 NKJV*

Paul informs all Christians that they should comfort one another with the hope of the resurrection of the dead and of the catching away of the resurrected dead and of "those who are alive and remain". We shall be "raptured" (caught up) to be with the Lord forever. *I*

Thessalonians 4:13-18 NKJV (see notes on Spirit, Soul, and Body, at the end of this book.)

RESPONSE:

Remind yourself that God has promised to give you joy in exchange for your grief; Know that grief is natural; freedom from grief is spiritual.

- Know that anointed Christian music can deliver you from grief.
- Talk with Christians who have been freed from grief.
- Expect God to hear your cry and remove the grief from you.

PERSONAL NOTES—CHAPTER 21

What is the exchange for grief?

_____

_____

What unexpected emotions can arise in a Christian because of grief?

_____

_____

_____

_____

In what ways can the pain of grief disrupt one's life?

_____

_____

_____

_____

What did Paul reveal in *I Thessalonians* that is intended to bring comfort?

_____

_____

_____

_____

List the contrast in the natural and the supernatural that pertains to grief.

_____

_____

_____

_____

When responding to grief and mourning, what three things can comfort the Christian?

_____

_____

_____

_____

EXCHANGE # 22

MY CHAINS OF BONDAGE FOR HIS LIBERTY

THEME SCRIPTURE:

ISAIAH 61:1-3— "The Spirit of the Lord God is upon Me, for He has anointed Me...to open the prison doors to those who are bound..." *NKJV*

ILLUSTRATION:

Jerry was a Christian. However, he had continual oppression from Satan and his agents. He could not understand why he still had problems with the devil. When he became a Christian, he thought that all of his problems would be behind him.

Jerry still had problems with sinful habits. He had a sickness that seemed resistant to all of the medicines that the doctor prescribed. He still experienced the bondage of fear. At times, the spirit of fear absolutely dominated his mind and emotions.

Finally, Jerry sought help by attending a seminar on healing and deliverance. During the prayer times, he witnessed the deliverances from oppression. He was afraid of the things that he saw and decided to leave. But a man with a microphone declared, "if you leave now, the demons will go with you. If you stay, God will free you from your demons."

Jerry went forward for prayer. He felt something that he had never felt before. He fell to his knees. Men spoke words over him, calling out demons. He was delivered of all of his bondages: spiritually, physically, mentally, emotionally, and financially.

Jerry was freed from every oppression—every bondage. He was free indeed.

TEACHING:

Jesus was the first to expel demons, freeing those who were bound. Everywhere He went while on Earth, He was doing good. *Acts 10:38 NKJV* He healed those who were sick, diseased, or disabled, and for those who were oppressed, He expelled the demons.

"...God anointed Jesus of Nazareth with the Holy Spirit and with power, Who went about doing good and healing all who were oppressed by the devil." *Acts 10:38 NKJV*

God does not want anyone to be bound. He offers liberty to everyone who has been imprisoned by the enemy. Jesus identified with you in every need. He represented you in every way. He went to the very bottom of every need that you will ever have. He can:

- Cleanse every stain.
- Heal every scar.
- Loose every shackle.
- Break every chain.
- Free every captive.

COST OF THIS BENEFIT:

All of the sins that control individuals were placed on Jesus, so that we could be free. While in the "lowest pit", He was exposed for three days and three nights by the demons of Hades, especially by Terror and Darkness. He cried to the Father, "You will not leave My soul in Hades, nor allow My body to see corruption." "You have laid Me in the lowest pit." "Terrors have destroyed me. All day long they surround me like a flood; they have completely engulfed Me." "My closest companion is Darkness." *Acts 2:17 NKJV; Psalms 16:10 Psalms 88:06; Psalms 88:16 NIV*

RESPONSE:

- Put off the old man which grows corrupt (wears out).
- Put on the new man created in Christ Jesus.
- Be renewed daily in your spirit (inner man).
- Develop the inner man continuously by spiritual exercises.
- Clothe yourself with the beauty that comes from within. *I Peter 3:04-05 NKJV*
- Build up your faith by praying in the Spirit; *Jude 20 KJV*
- Appropriate the promises in the Word by faith. *II Peter 1:03-04 NKJV*
- Expect the fruit of the Spirit to reside in your spirit. *Galatians 5:22-23 NKJV*

PERSONAL NOTES—CHAPTER 22:

Write the exchange that is listed in this chapter.

_____

_____

In *Acts 10:38, NKJV*, what activity did the writer reveal concerning Jesus?

_____

_____

_____

_____

List the five bullet points that may be needed in one's life in order to obtain liberty.

_____

_____

_____

_____

_____

_____

What was the cost for this exchange?

_____

_____

_____

_____

List the eight items that should be included in a Christian's response.

_____

_____

_____

_____

EXCHANGE # 23

MY TEMPORAL DESIRES FOR HIS ETERNAL PROMISES

THEME SCRIPTURE:

John 3:14-18 KJV— "...As Moses lifted up the serpent in the wilderness, even so must the Son of Man be lifted up, that whoever believes in Him should not perish, but have **eternal life**. (*17*) For God did not send His Son into the world to condemn the world, but that the world through Him might be saved. (*18*) He who believes in Him is not condemned; but he who does not believe is condemned already, because he has not believed in the name of the only begotten Son of God."

ILLUSTRATION:

A Youth Evangelist was attempting to explain the difference between the human life here on Earth verses eternity with the Lord. He used a single dot on a white board to represent a human life of 90 years. He then drew a line completely across the white board. Then he asked the young audience to imagine the line on the equator extending around the globe. He asked the audience if the demonstration gave them an accurate idea of eternal life.

NOTE: In order for this demonstration to be accurate, the line on the Equator would need to keep on circumventing the globe forever—eternally.

TEACHING:

Eternal—Greek word from which eternal is derived: *aionios*—means forever; everlasting.[20]

The Greek word, *aionios*, appears in the *New Testament* 46 times. It is translated everlasting 41 times. It is translated eternal 25 times.[17] This data implies that the two words are used interchangeably.[21]

MEDITATE ON THE ETERNAL:

There is an extraordinary fixation for temporary things. The desire to wear fashionable clothing; the need to possess the latest in footwear; the desire to be friends with the most popular students; the pride of driving a good-looking vehicle; the need of possessing things that your friends possess.

The fixation for temporary things can completely crowd out the desire for eternal things. I really like my car, but my car is not eternal. I really like my sports coats, but they are not eternal. They will eventually erode. I love my house, but it is not eternal. It often needs repair.

In contrast, there is a home prepared for me in Heaven that is eternal.

There is a great emphasis in America on the body. As one ages, the body begins to change—the body begins to wear out. It can no longer function as it once functioned.

One of the three basic youth conflicts is the emphasis on the temporal—the instant responses—the visible, the good tasting, the good feeling, the pleasant, the complementary words.[21]

Believers "walk by faith, not by sight." *II Corinthians 5:07 NKJV* "Therefore, we do not become discouraged. Though our outer self is wasting away, yet our inner self is being renewed day by day. For our momentary, light distress is producing for us an eternal weight of glory, beyond all measure (surpassing all comparisons, an endless blessedness). So, we look NOT AT THE THINGS WHICH ARE SEEN, BUT AT THE THINGS WHICH ARE UNSEEN; FOR THE THINGS WHICH ARE VISIBLE ARE TEMPORAL (JUST BRIEF AND FLEETING), BUT THE THINGS WHICH ARE INVISIBLE ARE EVERLASTING AND IMPERISHABLE." *II Corinthians 4:16-18 Amplified*

When the good news was circulated that Jesus was indeed alive, Thomas said "'Unless I see in His hands the print of the nails, and put my finger into the print of the nails, and put my hand into His side, I will not believe.'" Jesus said, "Thomas, blessed are those who have not seen, yet they believe." *John 20:25 NKJV*

Many Christians have the Thomas kind of faith—that is, a sense knowledge kind of faith. Unless I can see or feel or taste, I cannot believe.

COST OF THIS EXCHANGE:

Jesus chose to endure all of the sufferings involved in His sacrifice for us, for the joy that was before Him. *Hebrews 12:1-2 NKJV*

RESPONSE:

- I will seek the eternal things, especially love, joy, and peace.
- I choose rather to walk by faith and not by sight.
- I will believe the Word, especially when I cannot see the promised exchange.

PERSONAL NOTES—CHAPTER 23:

What is the meaning of the Greek word, *aionios*?

_____

_____

In what two ways is this word, aionios, translated?

_____

_____

_____

_____

What is one of the three Basic Youth Conflicts?

_____

_____

_____

_____

What is the encouraging word that is found in II Corinthians 4 that alerts us to the contrast of temporary and eternal?

_____

_____

_____

_____

What did Jesus tell Thomas in *John 20:25, NKJV*?

_____

_____

_____

_____

What was the cost for this exchange?

_____

_____

_____

_____

What are the three responses listed for this exchange?

_____

_____

_____

_____

EXCHANGE # 24

MY CONDEMNATION FOR FREEDOM IN CHRIST

THEME SCRIPTURES:

Romans 8:01— "There is therefore now no condemnation to those who are in Christ Jesus, who do not walk according to the flesh, but according to the Spirit. *KJV*

Romans 8:02— "For the law of the Spirit of life in Christ Jesus has freed me from the law of sin and death." *KJV*

ILLUSTRATION:

Hannah grew up in a denominational church that preached against girls wearing pants and using makeup. The preachers taught that it was a sin for Christians to dance, go to movie theaters, and attend sports events. They also taught that the youth of their denomination should only socialize with teens that were like-minded.

There was such an emphasis on sin that Hannah completed missed out on the freedom that Christ brings. She lived under a cloud of condemnation, due to the demands of the clergy to live a legalistic lifestyle.

When Hannah went to college, she attended a church that emphasized the grace of God. She witnessed the extraordinary difference in the lives of the youth and college age kids at the church.

Hannah desired to have that lifestyle demonstrated by the young people as well as the older people of the church. However, she had some difficulty in receiving the message of the grace of God and freedom in Christ.

The constant message of grace and truth over a four-year period brought the deliverance from religious tradition and legalism that Hannah needed so desperately.

DEFINITION:

Legalism: The direct or indirect attachment of behaviors, disciplines, and practices to the belief in order to achieve salvation and right standing before God, emphasizing a need to perform certain deeds in order to gain the promise of Heaven.[22] *The Christian Encyclopedia*

TEACHING:

There has been a tendency in every denomination to adopt a religious tradition. Over time, this tradition may take the place of grace and faith and the freedom that we enjoy through Christ. In his letters to the churches, Paul condemned witchcraft and legalism. He was much harsher to the church that moved back into legalism and the Law than he was to the church that moved into witchcraft.

It is so difficult to be delivered from religious spirits. It is difficult for a church to recognize that they have moved into legalism. If they recognize this fact, then the leadership must deal with a congregation that they have led into legalism. It is much more difficult to lead a congregation out of legalism, once they are captive to it.

As an individual Christian is taught that righteousness comes by religious acts or deeds, he/she adopts self-righteousness. This spiritual condition leads the individual to judge other Christians and non-Christians alike, especially those who are not acting exactly like he or she is acting. The judgmentalism leads to condemnation of all others who are not living like the legalistic Christian.

CONTRAST: JUDGE OR DISCERN:

"Judge not, lest you be judged." *Matthew 7:01 KJV* The Greek word for judge is **krino**.

Krino denotes judgment with a harshness, with a condemnation.[23]

Anakrino denotes discernment which denotes compassion and concern.[24]

Colossians 2:16-17— "Therefore, let no one judge you in regard to food and drink or in regard to [the observance of] a festival or a new moon or a Sabbath day. Such things are only a shadow of what is to come, and they have only symbolic value; but the substance (reality) of what is foreshadowed belongs to Christ." *Amplified*

I Corinthians 2:14-16 KJV— "But the natural man does not receive the things of the Spirit of God, for they are foolishness to him;

nor can he know them, because they are spiritually discerned. But he that is spiritual judges all things…" The Greek word translated "discerned" is *anakrino*.

RESPONSE:

- Resist the tendency to slide into religious rules and regulations.
- Embrace the grace of God that enables you to be what otherwise you could not be.
- Embrace the freedom that comes by living in the Word.
- Be led by your inner person (spirit), not by your soul.

PERSONAL NOTES—EXCHANGE 24:

Write the definition of legalism.

_____

_____

_____

_____

What has been the tendency in every denomination?

_____

_____

_____

_____

How does self-righteousness develop in a Christian's life?

_____

_____

_____

_____

Contrast "judge" and "discern".

_____

_____

_____

_____

Christians are alerted in "let no one judge us" in these five areas. List them.

_____

_____

_____

_____

What are the four responses listed for this exchange?

_____

_____

_____

_____

EXCHANGE # 25

MY LACK OF KNOWLEDGE FOR HIS REVELATION (RHEMA)

THEME SCRIPTURES:

As obedient children, do not be conformed to the former lusts which were yours in your ignorance..." *I Peter 1:14 KJV*

"...so that no advantage would be taken of us by Satan, for we are not ignorant of his schemes. *II Corinthians 2:11 NKJV*

"...My people are destroyed for lack of knowledge." *Hosea 4:06 KJV*

ILLUSTRATION:

Unfortunately, there are many people, even Christians, who sit in churches every Sunday without joy, peace, and satisfaction in their lives. This is mainly due to a lack of knowledge of the Word of God.

It is no longer okay for any Christian to live an unhappy, unfulfilled life. There is a wealth of good Bible teaching available on-line, that can be accessed by phone, IPAD, or computer. Every individual Christian is responsible to learn the truth from God's Word, so that he/she may possess righteousness, peace, and joy in the Holy Spirit.

Joe had been in Church most of his life. He had attended a Christian school, which required Bible class every day. However, after graduation from his school, he went away to college, and his life started to fall apart.

Joe had not been exposed to a systematic teaching of the spiritual concepts in the Word of God. Joe did not know who he was in Christ. Joe did not know the benefits that Jesus offers through His sacrifice. Joe did not possess the knowledge of the Word that would give him victory over the schemes of the enemy.

TEACHING:

The process of faith is explained in *Romans 10:17*: "So then faith comes by hearing, and hearing by the word of God." *NKJV*

CONTRAST OF *LOGOS* & *RHEMA*:

Logos is a Greek word translated as word; utterance; speech; reason. In *Strong's Exhaustive Concordance* it is # 3056.[25]

Rhema is a Greek word translated word; utterance; command or narration. In *Strong's* it is # 4487.[26]

Rhema is "the **word** that is near you. In your mouth and in your heart—that is the **word** of faith that we preach." *Romans 10:08 NKJV* Please note that the *rhema* word must be in both your mouth and your heart. Your speech (words) needs to be in agreement with the *rhema* **word** that is in your heart.

Rhema is the "faith that comes by hearing, and hearing by the **word** of God." *Romans 10:17 NKJV* Rhema *is that **word** that produces revelation. It is indeed the process that produces faith.*

Rhema is the "**Word** of God, which is the Sword of the Spirit." Therefore, *rhema* is one of the keys in "putting on the Full Armor of God, that you may be able to stand against the schemes of the Devil." *Ephesians 6:10 NKJV* When Jesus was tempted by Satan in the wilderness, Jesus used the Word of God to defeat him. Often Satan keeps harassing us until we use the Sword of the Spirit to drive him away.

THE KEY TO DISCIPLESHIP:

Jesus declared: "If you continue/abide/dwell in my word, then you will be my disciples." *John 8:31 NKJV* The word that is translated "continue" in the NKJV is *meno*$_{27}$ in the Greek language. It indicates a continuance in a place or in a relationship. It indicates abiding in the Word. It is a place of residence; it is where I live; it is where I dwell.

One cannot abide in the Word unless one knows the Word. This is just another opportunity to stress the study of the Word of God.

If you abide in His Word, "then you shall know the truth, and the truth will make you free." *John 8:31 NKJV*

RESPONSE:

As you study the Word of God (hopefully in a systematic manner), ask the Holy Spirit to be your teacher, guiding you into the truth, and causing the promises of God to become revelation in your heart and in your mind.

PERSONAL NOTES—EXCHANGE 25:

List the exchange featured in this chapter.

_____

_____

In *Hosea 4:6, KJV,* what was the cause of the destruction of God's people?

_____

_____

_____

_____

What is the meaning of the Greek word, *logos?*

_____

_____

_____

What is the meaning of the Greek word, *rhema?*

_____

_____

_____

_____

What two things must happen in a person's life in order for the "rhema" word to be effective in one's life?

_____

_____

_____

_____

How is faith produced in the life of a Christian, according to *Romans 10:17, KJV*?

_____

_____

_____

_____

What is the key to discipleship according to Jesus?

_____

_____

_____

_____

What should the believer do as he/she studies the Word of God?

_____

_____

_____

_____

EXCHANGE # 26

MY DEFEAT FOR HIS VICTORY (TRIUMPH)

THEME SCRIPTURE:

Colossians 2:15— "Having disarmed principalities and powers, He made a public spectacle of them, **triumphing** over them in it." *NKJV*

ILLUSTRATION:

Larry was an extraordinarily successful basketball player. However, something happened during his senior year in High School that would change him forever.

Larry had never been on a losing team. In fact, most of his teams had gone undefeated. After eighteen straight wins in his senior year, his team lost a game to a team that they had previously beaten.

It was not the loss that affected Larry so much, but the manner in which they lost. Larry could not arise to the challenge. Looking back, he had not played to his level of ability for several games. Years later, he would discover that he suffered from dehydration. During the game that actually affected him, he could not focus on the offense. He could not think. He could not deliver a safe pass. He could not hit his shots. He could not remember the plays. He slowly moved from offense to defense.

So, it was clear to Larry that it was his lack of play that cost his team the game. For the next several years, he could respond to others outwardly in a good way, but inwardly he had no confidence. He felt as if he was wearing a big sign that said, "LOSER". This losing attitude affected other areas of his life as well.

Something spiritual awakened Larry years later. He was tired of the inward feeling of being a loser. He developed a desire to be a "winner".

It was through this process that Larry learned that the only real way to win was to receive by faith the victory of Jesus over the forces of the enemy.

PAUL DEMONSTRATES THE COMPLETE AND AWESOME VICTORY OF JESUS BY THE ROMAN TRIUMPH:

- The Roman Emperor would assign a Roman General to conquer a city/nation.
- If the General was successful, the Roman Senate would declare a Triumph.
- Upon the General's return, he was welcomed with a parade.
- The General would lead the parade in a chariot pulled by white horses.

- Behind the General, the King of the conquered people would follow in chains.
- The conquered King's military officers were also in chains.
- Next in the parade would be the prime animals, housed in cages.
- Gold, silver, and precious stones would be displayed on wagons.
- Wagons loaded with recently harvested crops would follow.
- The finest animals chosen from the herds and flocks of the conquered nation would finish the parade.[28]

The Triumph would publicly demonstrate the complete victory over the conquered nation.

HOW DID JESUS TRIUMPH:

Jesus had spent three days and three nights in Hades, the place for departed souls. Satan's agent by the name of Hades, was the keeper of this place for departed souls.

When Jesus had fulfilled every detail in the sacrificial plan of God, God justified Him in His spirit. Jesus then became the first individual to be born again in His Spirit. Jesus became the first individual to exchange His sin nature for righteousness.

Then Jesus began a march through Hades, capturing the agents of Satan, disarming the principalities and powers, making a public spectacle of them, (*Colossians 2:15 NKJV*) for all of Heaven and Hades to witness. Then He took the keys to Death and Hades. *Revelations 1:18 KJV* He triumphed over them! He stripped Satan and all of his agents of their weapons, and offered to believers His mighty weapons. Satan is not as powerful as he once was in the Old Covenant. He was defeated by Jesus. You can administer that defeat in your life by faith. This was indeed an awesome and complete TRIUMPH.

COST OF THIS EXCHANGE:

First Jesus had to descend into the lower parts of the Earth, so that He could ascend. He first had to be placed in the hands of principalities and powers of the enemy, so that He could break through and triumph over them, making a public spectacle of Satan and his agents. *Ephesians 4:09 NKJV*

RESPONSE:

- Speak and sing to yourself in Psalms and Hymns and spiritual songs.
- Remind yourself daily that you are "blessed".
- Be constantly aware that "old things (habits) are passed away, all things are new, all things are of God."
- Treat negative thoughts and words as your enemy.
- Make a commitment that you are a winner with Jesus.
- Picture all of your enemies in chains behind the chariot of Jesus.
- Administer the defeat of Satan by Jesus through faith.

Make sure that, in the triumphal parade of Jesus, you are not merely on the sidelines cheering. You need to be in the chariot with Jesus, dragging the defeated agents of Satan behind the chariot in chains.

PERSONAL NOTES—EXCHANGE 26:

What is the title of the exchange that is featured in this chapter?

_____

_____

What event did Paul use to describe the victory of Jesus over principalities and powers of the enemy?

_____

_____

What did Jesus do after God justified Him and raised Him in His spirit?

_____

_____

_____

_____

What was the cost of this exchange?

_____

_____

_____

_____

What should be the response of the Christian to this exchange?

_____

_____

_____

_____

_____

_____

EXCHANGE # 27

MY IMAGINATIONS FOR HIS SPIRITUAL WEAPONS

THEME SCRIPTURE:

"For though we live in the world, we are not carrying on a worldly war: For the weapons of our warfare are not earthly, but are mighty through God for the pulling down of strongholds, casting down imaginations, and reasonings, bringing every thought captive to the obedience of Christ." *II Corinthians 10:3-5 NKJV*

ILLUSTRATION:

Darryl was a teenager that lived in the Northwest part of the US. Every Sunday, he would help his two younger brothers to get dressed, so that he could walk them the 6 blocks to the Sunday morning church service. Darryl and his brothers attended almost every Sunday for 3 years.

In his junior year in High School, he was exposed to an English teacher who was a gifted speaker. The goal of this instructor was to free the Christian students from their belief that the Bible was the true inspired Word of God. Often, he would question the miracles listed in the Bible, asking specific questions; "Do you really believe that Jonah spent 3 days in the belly of a whale, was then spit out onto the shore, and went and preached to the people of Nineveh? Do you really believe that Jesus was born of a virgin? Do you really believe that Jesus died and rose from the dead after 3 days?

After weeks and months of the questions, reasonings, and arguments, Darryl no longer was a believer. He, in fact, began to repeat the reasonings of that instructor.

Darryl and his brothers never came back to our church or any other church.

TEACHING:

A great many Church members have become captives of vain imaginations that lead to worry and fear. A great many Christian teens have attended universities and have been persuaded by ungodly reasonings and philosophies, trading their childlike faith for an agnostic opinion.

A vital part of the equipping of the saints must include the knowledge of spiritual warfare and the acknowledgement of spiritual weapons. Jesus not only disarmed principalities and powers, stripping the weapons from Satan and his agents, but He also armed His believers with weapons that are "mighty through God". *I Corinthians 10:3-5 NKJV*

HOW MIGHTY ARE YOUR SPIRITUAL WEAPONS?

- Pulling down strongholds of the enemy.
- Casting down imaginations, worry, fear.
- Casting down reasonings and every high thing that exalts itself against the Word of God.
- Bringing every thought into obedience to Christ.
- Bind the strong man (enemy) and release those who are bound.

Paul reveals to us that our spiritual weapons are so mighty that they will pull down the strongholds of the enemy.

IDENTIFYING YOUR SPIRITUAL WEAPONS:

- THE NAME OF JESUS
- THE WORD OF GOD
- THE BLOOD OF JESUS

HOW DOES THE BELIEVER ACTIVATE THE WEAPONS?

- Prayer-the Word of God; prayer in the Name of Jesus; declarations in the Name of Jesus.
- Praise-the Name of Jesus. Testify (confess) to what the Blood of Jesus has done for you.
- Teaching—the Word; the identity of the believer; what Jesus purchased for us.

COST OF THIS BENEFIT:

When Jesus was tempted by the devil in the wilderness, Satan approached Him with reasonings. When the soul of Jesus went to Hades, the place of the dead, He was surrounded by terror and darkness. He was tempted by imaginations and reasonings. Every demon in Hades was questioning His faith in the Father.

Imaginations would have resounded in His mind and in His emotions. He was identifying with us in our needs.

RESPONSE:

- Make a decision "to win the spiritual warfare".
- Cast down imaginations in the mighty Name of Jesus.
- Bring every bad thought captive to the obedience of Christ.
- Launch the mighty Name of Jesus against the ungodly education system.
- Declare on behalf of your kids and grandkids, "No weapon formed against them shall prosper." *Isaiah 54:17 KJV*

PERSONAL NOTES—EXCHANGE 27:

List the title of the exchange in this chapter.

_____

_____

What are four effects that testify to the power of your spiritual weapons?

_____

_____

_____

_____

What are the three major spiritual weapons that must be used by Christians?

_____

_____

_____

How does the believer activate these weapons?

_____

_____

_____

_____

What was the cost of this benefit?

_____

_____

_____

_____

What should be the response to this exchange?

_____

_____

_____

_____

_____

_____

_____

EXCHANGE # 28

MY WEAKNESS FOR HIS POWER

THEME SCRIPTURE:

"So now I am glad to boast about my weaknesses, so that the power of Christ can work ... And He said unto me, 'My grace is sufficient for you': for My strength is made perfect ... in distresses for Christ's sake: for when I am weak, then I am strong." *I Corinthians 12:09 NKJV*

"I can do all things through Christ Who strengthens me." *Philippians 4:13 KJV*

ILLUSTRATION:

The fans of a certain high school basketball team had gathered in the lobby of the gymnasium, waiting for the players to come out of the locker room. I, also, was waiting to congratulate the players on a game well played.

When the players appeared in the lobby, my attention immediately went to the game shoes of one of the players. I could not make out the writing, but on closer inspection, I saw that it was an acronym: I C D A T T C W S M. I asked, "what do the letters represent?" He replied, "I can do all things through Christ who strengthens me." He continued the explanation, "Every time that I shoot a free throw, I bounce the ball, look down and see the acronym. It reminds me of the basis for my faith and my confidence."

I stated to him, "What a great testimony of the ways in which Jesus can help Christians."

That player was my son, Clint. It was a part of his testimony throughout his basketball career.

POWER THROUGH THE WORD:

"For the word of God is living and active, sharper than any two-edged sword, piercing to the division of soul and of spirit, of joints and of marrow, and discerning the thoughts and intentions of the heart." *Hebrews 4:12 NKJV* The Word of God is the only means to determine the division of the spirit and the soul of man/woman. If it were not for this remarkable division, many Christians would continue to live for God in a soulish manner—not in a spiritual manner. Some ministers would continue to preach and teach in a soulish manner, living in a soulish way.

"For I am not ashamed of **the** Gospel (good news) of Christ, for it **is** God's power working unto salvation [for deliverance from eternal death] to everyone who believes..." *Romans 1:16 NKJV*

"The Gospel is the power of God unto salvation (deliverance)." *Romans 1:16 KJV* The Gospel of Jesus Christ has the ability and power to deliver men, women, boys, and girls from the grip of habits, from the chains of addiction, and from the prison of oppression.

POWER IN THE NAME:

Because of Jesus' sacrifice, God gave Him the most powerful Name there is: "And being found in human form, he humbled Himself by becoming obedient to the point of death, even death on a cross. Therefore, God has highly exalted Him and bestowed on Him the Name that is above every Name, so that at the Name of Jesus every knee should bow, in heaven and on earth and under the earth, and every tongue confess that Jesus Christ is Lord, to the glory of God the Father." *Philippians 2:08-11 NKJV*

The Holy Spirit has enlightened you:

"So that you may know:

- The hope of His calling.
- The riches of His inheritance in the saints.
- The exceeding greatness of His power toward us who believe—

According to the working of His mighty power, which He worked in Christ when He raised Him from the dead and seated Him at His right hand in the Heavenly places, far above all principality and power and might and dominion, and every name that is named, not only in this age but also in the age to come." *Ephesians 1:18-21 KJV*

Note the direction of God's mighty power: His mighty resurrection power is towards us who believe. The same power that He used to raise Jesus from the dead, He offers to us.

POWER IN THE BLOOD:

"And they overcame him (Satan) by the blood of the Lamb, and by the word of their testimony, and they loved not their lives unto the death." Revelation 12:11 KJV

POWER TO WITNESS:

"And you shall receive power after the Holy Spirit has come upon you, and you shall be witnesses unto Me…" Acts 1:08 KJV Every Christian has the experience of forgiveness of sins—the new birth—that can be related to others. This is a witness as to what Jesus has done for you.

BELIEVERS ARE EMPOWERED:

"These signs shall follow those who believe: In My mane they will cast out demons; they will speak with new tongues; ….they will lay hands on the sick and they shall recover."

Mark 16:17-18 KJV

COST OF THIS EXCHANGE:

When God made Jesus to be sin, Jesus was stripped of His righteousness. From that moment forward, He was totally alone. He experienced the remainder of His sacrifices without the power of Heaven and without the union with His Father.

RESPONSE:

Acknowledge: I will never be able to withstand the strategies and manipulations of my enemy without the POWER of Almighty God. Furthermore, I will never be able to fulfill God's assignment for me, except by moving and living and having my being in Him and

His power. However, as a believer in His Word, I have His promise that His power is toward us who believe. This power is defined as the same power that raised Jesus from the dead. I have the promise of the One Who cannot lie and cannot fail, that He gives to me, a believer, **this same power.**

PERSONAL NOTES—EXCHANGE 28:

What is the exchange that God offers to us that is featured in this chapter?

_____

_____

Describe the uniqueness of the Word of God.

_____

_____

_____

_____

What three things are listed in the Word about which the Holy Spirit enlightens the believer?

_____

_____

_____

_____

What is the measure of the power that God directs toward the believer?

_____

_____

According to *Revelations 12:11, KJV,* how do Christians in this time period overcome Satan?

_____

_____

EXCHANGE # 29

MY JUDGMENTALISM FOR HIS DISCERNMENT

THEME SCRIPTURE:

I Corinthians 2:09—12 KJV: "But it is written: 'Eye has not seen, nor ear heard, nor has entered into the heart of man the things which God has prepared for those who love Him.'"

ILLUSTRATION:

JT was a successful businessman with a wide circle of friends. He had so many friends due to his outgoing personality and his gift of hospitality. He was ready at any time to help any of his friends who needed his help.

A story about J T was told by an individual who was motivated by jealousy. Before long, the story circulated throughout J T's circle of friends.

J T's friends suddenly changed towards him. He felt the animosity coming from both good friends and casual acquaintances. J T was shut out of group activities and fellowship meetings. After a steady diet of this treatment, J T gave up trying to be a part of the group.

J T did not allow this incident to affect him spiritually or emotionally. God sent him new friends.

Twelve years passed, and the story was proven to be false. J T had lost many good friends because of the lies—some of the friends were lifetime friends. Those lifetime friends had lost twelve years of blessed fellowship with J T.

J T's former friends had been Christians. Most of them claimed to be believers. Whenever one of his former friends would approach him to apologize, he would accept the apology gracefully, and then ask: "Where was your discernment?"

THE REVELATION OF GIFTS, BLESSINGS, AND BENEFITS:

"But God has revealed them to us through His Spirit. For the Spirit searches all things, yes, the deep things of God." *I Corinthians 2:10 NKJV*

MAN/WOMAN CANNOT KNOW HIMSELF/HERSELF???

"For what man knows the things of a man except the spirit of the man which is in him? Even so, no man knows the things of God except the Spirit of God." *I Corinthians 2:11 NKJV*

THE SPIRIT OF THE WORLD VS THE SPIRIT OF GOD:

"Now we have received, not the spirit of the world, but the Spirit Who is from God, that we might know the things that have been freely given to us by God." *I Corinthians 2:12 NKJV*

THE DEVELOPMENT OF THE INNER MAN:

"And He gave some as apostles, and some as prophets, and some as evangelists, and some as pastors and teachers, for the equipping of the saints for the work of service, to the building up of the body of Christ; until we all attain to the unity of the faith, and of the knowledge of the Son of God, **to a mature man, to the measure of the stature which belongs to the fullness of Christ.**" *Ephesians 4:11-12 KJV*

The inner man receives:

- The revelation of the Word by the Holy Spirit; *Romans 10:17 NKJV*
- The nature of righteousness, replacing sin-consciousness; *II Corinthians 5:21 NKNV*
- The eternal life of God, replacing eternal separation from God; *I John 5:12 NKJV*
- Pastors and teachers as gifts from the Lord to equip you for discipleship. *Ephesians 4:11-12; John 8:31 NKJV*
- An abundance of grace, so that you may abound in good works. *II Corinthians 9:08 NKJV*

RESPONSE:

- Build up your spirit (inner person), so that you may discern spiritual matters.

- Expose your soul continuously to the Word of God, so that your spirit will have ascendency in your life.
- Meditate on "who you are in Christ" and those benefits that you possess through Him.
- Meditate on the promises of God.

PERSONAL NOTES—EXCHANGE 29:

What is the title of the exchange that is featured in this chapter?

_____

_____

List five things that are received in the inner man (spirit).

_____

_____

_____

_____

_____

What was the purpose for which Jesus gave the gifts listed in *Ephesians chapter 4*?

_____

_____

_____

What are four responses for the believer to this exchange?

_____

_____

_____

_____

EXCHANGE # 30

MY UNHEALTHINESS
FOR HIS HEALTH

THEME SCRIPTURE:

III John 3:2—"I wish above all things that you prosper and be in health, even as your soul prospers." *KJV*

ILLUSTRATION:

Two young ministers were in a friendly debate concerning God's provision for healing and health. David believed that God provided not only healing for all sicknesses, but also extended to believers the provision of divine health.

Jim stated that divine health meant that we could have the health of God. "No way is that ever happening. That is just too much to believe."

David replied, "God offers to us His own righteousness. He extends to us the gift of eternal life, which is His own life. He offers to us His blessing, and when He showers favor upon us, it is His own favor. When He gives us health, it is His own health."

Jim stated that he could not ever believe that unless he saw it in a Scripture.

David had no Scriptural evidence, so the debate was concluded.

Twelve years later, David discovered the Scriptural evidence: "MY TENDENCY TO BE SICK FOR HIS HEALTH."

GOD'S DESIRE FOR YOU:

3 John 2— "I wish above all things that you prosper and be in health, even as your soul prospers." *KJV*

1 Peter 2:24— "…and by His stripes (wounds) you were healed (past tense)." *NKJV*

TEACHING:

The soul that prospers means:

- The mind has been and continues to be renewed through the Word of God.
- The emotions have been placed under the control of the Word and of the Holy Spirit.
- The will has conformed to the will of God and His plan for your life.

THE EXTRAORDINARY PRICE FOR YOUR HEALTH:

"The whole head is sick—the whole heart faints—from the sole of the foot even to the head, there is no soundness (health) in it—only wounds and bruises and putrefying sores. They have not been closed or bound up, or soothed with ointment." *Isaiah 1:5-6 NKJV*

* This is the picture of rebellion as God sees it.
* It is the picture of Jesus on the cross.
* "I wish above all things that you prosper and be in health." *III John 2 NKJV*

PROVISION FOR HEALING AND HEALTH:

God has provided everything that we need in this life and the life to come through His grace. We will study in this lesson the way in which God has done this through Jesus.

* God put all of our sicknesses and diseases on Jesus. He bore our griefs and sorrows, and carried our physical needs. Peter not only quotes Isaiah, but also gives us the revelation that the healing of our sicknesses and diseases has already been paid for by Jesus.

    "Surely He has borne our griefs and carried our sorrows, but we did esteem Him stricken, smitten of God. And we hid our faces from Him."

    But He was wounded for our transgressions; He was bruised for our iniquities; The chastisement of our peace was upon Him; and by His stripes we are healed." *Isaiah 53:3-4* (Prophecy concerning Jesus) *Matthew 8:17 NKJV*— "He Himself took our infirmities and bore our sicknesses."

1 Peter 2:24 KJV— "...and by His stripes (wounds) you were (past tense) healed."

In *Isaiah, chapter one (NKJV),* the prophet is describing the spiritual condition of the nation of Israel. They have been in rebellion against God, and under the law, the picture of rebellion is stated here by Isaiah: "The whole head is sick...there is no soundness in the body...only bleeding and sores and putrefying flesh."

God's desire for His covenant people was not only to provide healing for every infirmity, but also to provide through His Son Jesus, divine health. Therefore, Jesus, Who knew no sickness, became sick by identifying with our sicknesses. Jesus, Who never had a disease, became diseased by identifying with our diseases. Jesus, Who had never rebelled against God, paid the price for our rebellion, bearing the consequences for our rebellion by identifying with our tendency to be sick, so that we could be free from the tendency to be sick—thus enjoying the desire of God for us—that is, to live in health.

In this provision for us, there was no health at all in the body of Jesus. No wonder that historians write concerning His crucifixion that "He was not recognizable as a human being."

RESPONSE:

Realize that the benefits of divine health and prosperity are conditional on the prosperity of the SOUL—(my mind, my emotions, and my will). The soul can only prosper by the renewing of the mind through the word of God. It is a continuous process that must be observed throughout this earthly life. My emotions must be retrained, so that they do not dictate to me how I react to others when they mistreat me or when they have differing opinions than I have. My relationship with my family and friends is too important for me to respond to them emotionally.

I commit my soul to be transformed by the Word of God. I commit to renew my mind through His Word. I commit to retrain my emotions through His Word and His Spirit. I commit to conform my will to the will of God. In this manner, my soul begins to prosper.

Jesus commitment to His Father, God: "Lo I have come to do Your will; I find Your will in the volume of the book." *Hebrews 10:7-10 NKJV* In the same manner, I will find His purpose and His will for me in His WORD.

PERSONAL NOTES—EXCHANGE 30:

List the title of the exchange that is featured in this chapter?

_____

_____

What is God's desire for every believer that is revealed in *III John 2, KJV*?

_____

_____

_____

_____

What must happen in order for your soul to prosper?

_____

_____

_____

_____

What is the picture of rebellion that God sees that is revealed in *Isaiah chapter 1, NKJV*?

_____

_____

_____

_____

What was the cost of providing this benefit to Christians?

_____

_____

_____

_____

#31 EXCHANGE

MY VULNERABILITY FOR HIS PROTECTION

THEME SCRIPTURE:

"I will say of the Lord, 'He is my refuge and my fortress; My God, in Him I will trust.'" *Psalms 91:02 NKJV*

ILLUSTRATION:

John Lake writes about an experience that he had in Africa in the 1930s. The Bubonic Plague had touched many parts of Africa. Lake and his associates came upon a village in which every resident had died of the plague. As they were in the process of burying the dead, a medical team from the U S Army arrived.

The doctor warned Lake of the danger of contacting this deadly disease. Lake asked if the virus was still alive in the recent dead tribesmen. The doctor replied that it was certainly the case.

Lake asked the doctor to take an infected specimen from a tribesman and place it under the microscope, in order to verify that the virus was still alive. Then he placed the specimen on his open hand, placed his hand under the microscope, and viewed that the virus had immediately died.

Lake then explained to the doctor that his faith in the life of God that lived within him would not allow the virus to affect his body.[30]

The life of God within Lake protected him from the virus.

TEACHING:

PROTECTION FROM EVIL & PLAGUES:

"Because you have made the Lord [Who is my refuge], even the Most High, your dwelling place, no evil will befall you, nor will any plague come near your dwelling." *Psalms 91:09 NKJV*

ANGELIC PROTECTION:

"For He will command His angels in regard to you, to protect and defend and guard you in all your ways." *Psalms 91:11 NKJV*

Perhaps the best illustration of this angelic protection in the Old Testament is of the prophet, Elisha, and his administrative assistant: (*From II Kings 8:18 NKJV*) The King of Syria desired to make war against Israel. Whenever he made plans to attack them, Elisha would reveal those plans to the King of Israel, thus thwarting the Syrian plans. The King of Syria asked his servants, "Who among us is revealing our plans of war to Israel? No one, my Lord, O King, but Elisha tells the King of Israel the words that you speak in secret."

The King of Syria sent his army during the night to surround the city where Elisha dwelt. Elisha's assistant, seeing the great Syrian army, said to Elisha, "Alas, my master, what shall we do?" Elisha answered, "Don't be afraid, for those who are with us are greater than those who are with them."

Elisha then asked the Lord to open his servant's eyes that he might see. When that occurred, the servant saw that the mountain was filled with horses and chariots of fire all around Elisha.

Elisha, his assistant, and the Israelites were protected that day from a mighty Syrian army that sought to conquer them.

PROTECTION IN THE NIGHT:

Psalms 91:5-6 NKJV—"You shall not be afraid of the terror by night, nor of the arrow that flies by day, nor of the pestilence that walks in darkness, nor of the destruction that lays waste at noonday."

PRAYER FOR THE STORM:

In the dark of the midnight have I oft hid my face;

While the storm howls above me, and there's no hiding place.

'Mid the crash of the thunder, Precious Lord, hear my cry—

Keep me safe till the storm passes by.[31] Mosie Lister

RESPONSE:

I will <u>say</u> of the Lord, "He is my refuge and my fortress—my God—in Him, I will trust." *Psalms 91:02 NKJV* I will activate the 'word of faith' which is in my heart <u>and</u> in my mouth. *Romans 10:08 NKJV* I will resist the devil and he will flee from me. By faith, I will activate my spiritual weapons: The Name of Jesus; The Word of God; The Blood of Jesus. I will walk in safety, for I know that the angels are protecting me from all harm.

PERSONAL NOTES—EXCHANGE 31:

What is the exchange that is featured in this chapter?

_____

_____

What are the two effects that are listed in *Psalms 91:09, NKJV*?

_____

_____

_____

What are the four results of making the Lord your refuge (*Psalms 91:5-6, NKJV*)?

_____

_____

_____

_____

What is the promise in *Psalms 91, NKJV*, concerning the angels?

_____

_____

_____

What should be the response of Christians to this exchange?

_____

_____

_____

_____

_____

_____

_____

32 EXCHANGE

MY DARKNESS
FOR HIS LIGHT

THEME SCRIPTURE:

"You are a chosen race, a royal priesthood, a holy nation, God's own people, in order that you may proclaim the mighty acts of him who called you out of **darkness** into **his marvelous light**."*1 Peter 2:09 NKJV*

ILLUSTRATION:

Janice had grown up regularly attending church. She had Christian parents. She remembered singing in Kids' Church, *This little light of mine—I'm gonna let it shine*. But she felt that her light was not being seen by anyone.

Janice talked with a lady on the worship team about her dilemma. "I'm not a singer nor a speaker. What can I do to let my light shine?"

The lady asked her if she had ever witnessed to anyone about her experience with the Lord. She further explained, "anyone who is a Christian should be able to tell someone about their conversion. You should take the following steps:"

"Write out exactly how you felt the need of becoming a Christian. Then write about the moment that you were converted. Then write what this experience has meant to you in your life and your family. Then practice saying it in front of a mirror. Then let the Holy Spirit lead you to individuals who need to hear your testimony."

Janice followed this advice and became a witness for the Lord. Her light was shining!

TEACHING:

JESUS IS THE LIGHT:

Jesus declared, "I am the light of the world; he who follows Me will not walk in the darkness, but will have the Light of life." *John 8:12 NKJV*

"For He rescued us from the domain of darkness, and transferred us to the kingdom of His beloved Son." *Colossians 1:13 NKJV*

PAUL CALLED TO MINISTER TO THE JEWS AND THE GENTILES:

Jesus appeared to Paul on the Damascus Road to make him a minister to the Jews and the Gentiles. "...I now send you to open their eyes, in order to turn them from **darkness to light,** and from the power of Satan to God, that they may receive forgiveness of sins

and an inheritance among those who are sanctified by faith in Me."
Acts 26:17-18 NKJV

DARKNESS REPRESENTS SPIRITUAL IGNORANCE:

"And this is the condemnation, that light is come into the world, and
men loved darkness rather than light, because their deeds were
evil. For everyone practicing evil hates the light, and does not come
to the light, lest his deeds should be exposed." John 3:19-20 NKJV

In Him was life, and the life was the light of men. The light shines
in the darkness, and the darkness did not comprehend it." *John
1:4-5 NKJV*

CHRISTIANS ARE NOT OF THE NIGHT NOR OF DARKNESS:

But you, brethren, are not in darkness, that the day would overtake
you like a thief; for you are all **sons of light and sons of day.** We are
not of night nor of darkness. *1 Thessalonians 5:4-5 NKJV*

"I have come as Light into the world, so that everyone who believes
in Me will not remain in darkness." *John 12:46 NKJV*

"But the path of the righteous is like the shining sun, that shines ever
brighter unto the perfect day." *Proverbs 4:18 NKJV*

JESUS PROCLAIMS THAT CHRISTIANS ARE THE LIGHT OF THE WORLD:

"You are the light of the world. A city that is set on a hill cannot be
hidden. Nor do they light a lamp and put it under a basket, but on
a lampstand, and it gives light to all who are in the house. Let your
light so shine before men, that they may see your good works and
glorify your Father in Heaven." *Matthew 5:14-16 NKJV*

Jesus finished His work here on Earth, having sacrificed Himself by representing us in every human need that we would ever have. He announced to His disciples, "I'm returning to My Father. I'm placing My work—the work of the Kingdom of God—in your hands" This was His plan A. There was no plan B. The future of the Church was now in the hands of His disciples.

RESPONSE:

"I believe that, because of the work of Jesus in my life, I am a light to a dark world. I trust the Holy Spirit to enlighten me and guide me, as I commit to being that light. Because I am the righteousness of God in Christ, my path will grow brighter and brighter."

PERSONAL NOTES—EXCHANGE 32:

List the title of the exchange that is featured in this chapter.

_____

_____

What was the declaration that Jesus revealed in *John 8:12, NKJV*?

_____

_____

_____

_____

What two things did Jesus do for us that is revealed in *Colossians 1:13, NKJV*?

_____

_____

_____

_____

What does darkness represent?

_____

_____

_____

_____

What did Jesus expect concerning light?

_____

_____

_____

_____

#33 EXCHANGE

MY WEARINESS
FOR HIS REST

THEME SCRIPTURE:

"Come to Me, all of you who are weary and heavy laden, and I will give you rest." *Matthew 11:28 KJV*

ILLUSTRATION:

"I'm so tired! I do not know what to do. I am so tired that I cannot even think. I'm sick and tired of being sick and tired!"

Louis is a businessman. His business has quickly grown. He now has 23 employees. He works long hours. Even when he leaves his business in the early evening, he cannot stop thinking about his business trends and planning his next project. He often takes the problems of his business to his home—to his family.

Louis loves his family and desires to spend meaningful time with them. However, he feels trapped by his commitment to his business and to his employees. He is needed every day—every hour of every day—by his employees.

Louis was invited to a men's breakfast by his neighbor. He thought of excuses in order to get out of it without offending his neighbor. In the end, Louis attended the breakfast.

It was not a minister who spoke at the breakfast. It was an ordinary businessman, much like Louis. The man told of the exact situation that Louis was in.

Something inside Louis began to stir. The speaker explained that he had become desperate, looking for a solution. He eventually came to a place that he cried out to God for help. He felt much better, but still there was no solution. He read a book by E W Kenyon, concerning an inner peace and a spiritual rest. He read the book several times, so that he could understand how to establish this experience in his own life.

When the breakfast was over, Louis stood with a few men, waiting to talk with the speaker. As Louis shook hands with the speaker, the speaker was drawn to him and said, "you must be the one that I was talking to this morning."

He gave Louis the book by E W Kenyon that explained the spiritual rest and inner peace that was available to every believer. The two men established a day in which they could meet for breakfast each week to discuss this experience.

Louis thanked God for this encounter. He experienced the worry and stress melt away. He became a spiritual force for his family and for his employees. God had intervened in his life. The Exchange, My stress for His spiritual rest, certainly worked for Louis.

EXPECTATION—A COMPONENT PART OF FAITH:

"Even youths grow tired and weary, and young men stumble and fall; but those who wait upon the Lord will renew their strength. They will soar on wings like eagles; they will run and not grow weary; they will walk and not be faint." *Isaiah 40:30-31 NKJV*

Definition: the Hebrew word that is translated "wait" is *quavah,* meaning to expect; to hope for; to wait; to look for.[32] Perhaps a more accurate translation of this word would be: "...those who wait expectantly on the Lord shall renew their strength..."

SPIRITUAL REST:

"Take My yoke upon you and learn from Me, for I am gentle and humble in heart, and you will find rest for your soul. Matthew 11:39 NKJV

This exchange, that is offered to us by Jesus, is an inner peace—a place of spiritual rest:

*Rest from worry, unbelief, and doubt;
*Rest from pain and suffering;
*Rest from confusion and strife;
*Rest from stress and anxiety;
*Rest from fear and terror.

"Therefore, we do not become discouraged, though our outer self is progressively wasting away, yet our inner self is being progressively renewed day by day. For our momentary, light distress is producing for us an eternal weight of glory beyond all measure, surpassing all comparisons, a transcendent splendor and an endless blessedness. So, we look not at things which are visible, but at the things which are not visible; for the things which are visible are temporal [brief and fleeting], but the things which are invisible are everlasting and imperishable." *II Corinthians 4:16-18 Amplified*

Hebrews 4:1-3 NKJV— "Therefore, while the promise of entering His rest still remains and is freely offered today, let us fear, in case any one of you may seem to come short of reaching it or think he has come too late. For we who believe enter that rest..."

RESPONSE:

Hebrews 12:1-03 NKJV: **RUN THE RACE WITH ENDURANCE:**

- Strip off every unnecessary weight.
- Rid yourself of each sin that entangles you.
- Look away from all that will distract you.
- Focus your eyes upon Jesus.
- Meditate on Him Who endured bitter hostilities for you.
- As a result, you will not grow weary and lose heart.

PERSONAL NOTES—EXCHANGE 33:

What is the title of the exchange that is featured in this chapter?

_____

_____

What was the instruction of Jesus that would bring rest to the soul?

_____

_____

_____

What five statements describe this spiritual rest that Jesus offers?

_____

_____

_____

_____

_____

_____

In Hebrews, _chapter 4, Amplified_, what assurance is featured that convinces believers that this rest is available, even in a pandemic?

_____

_____

_____

_____

What are five responses that those who seek this rest should employ?

_____

_____

_____

_____

AFTERTHOUGHTS:
SPIRIT, SOUL, AND BODY:

PROLOGUE: SPIRIT, SOUL, BODY:

Pneuma— (Greek word) =spirit—*Strong's # 4151.*[32]

"...the Lord, Who stretches out the heavens, lays the foundation of the earth, and forms the spirit of man within him." *Zechariah 12:01 NKJV*

Another translation reads, "...formed a spirit in the midst of man." *Zechariah 12:1 KJV*

God created man as a spirit being, gave him a soul, and housed him in a body.

When God breathed into Adam, his spirit (inner man) filled his body, much like the air fills a balloon and takes on the shape of that specific balloon.

He placed man (Adam) in the Garden of Eden and made a companion for him (Eve). God gave Adam dominion over the Earth with one restriction: "But (only) from the tree of the knowledge (recognition) of good and evil you shall not eat, for in the day that you eat of it, you shall certainly die." *Genesis 2:17 Amplified*

Satan entered the garden and deceived Eve, who ate of the forbidden tree. Later, Adam joined her in the disobedience. That very day Adam died in his spirit. His fellowship with God was cut off. He was driven from the garden. His nature was changed from righteousness to a sinful nature.

When Adam sinned, everyone sinned. His sinful nature was inherited by every generation that followed. Paul stated, "For as by one man's disobedience, many were made sinners, so also by one Man's obedience, many will be made righteous." *Romans 5:19 NKJV*

NEW BIRTH:

Thus, mankind inherited from Adam a sinful nature and a spirit that was dead in trespasses and sins. "And you He made alive, who were dead in trespasses and sins." *Ephesians 2:1 NKJV*

THE SPIRIT MUST BE BORN AGAIN:

Jesus answered Nicodemus, "Most assuredly I say unto you, unless one is born again, he cannot see the kingdom of God...unless one is born of water and the Spirit, he cannot enter the kingdom of God." *John 3:3-5 NKJV*

SOUL—MIND, WILL, EMOTIONS:

Psuche is the Greek word for soul.

Psuche— (Greek word)—soul—*Strong's # 5590*=mind, will, and emotions.[33]

Whereas the spirit of man must be born again, the soul of man must be transformed—radically changed. To accomplish this, the mind must be renewed, the will must conform to the will of God, and the emotions must be retrained.

MIND:

Romans 12:2: "Be not be conformed to this world, but be transformed by the renewing of your mind, so that you may be able to prove the good, the acceptable, and the perfect will of God." *NKJV*

God said, "My thoughts are not your thoughts nor are your ways my ways. For as the heavens are higher than the earth, so are My ways higher than your ways, and My thoughts than your thoughts." *Isaiah 55:8-9 NKJV*

God is saying, "You don't think like I think. Our thoughts are incompatible. You need to change the way that you think. In order for you to change your thinking, you must submit your mind to my Word."

The mind has been called by many Bible teachers a battlefield. *II Corinthians 10:3-5 KJV:* "For though we walk in the flesh, we do not war according to the flesh. For the weapons of our warfare are not carnal (earthly), but mighty in God:"

- Pulling down strongholds (of the enemy)
- Casting down imaginations
- Casting down reasonings
- Bringing every thought captive to the obedience of Christ.

Thoughts, reasonings, and imaginations are produced by the mind. This is the area where most of the battles with the enemy of believers take place.

NOTE: The effective use of the spiritual weapons will be taught in much more detail in a Bible course entitled "Spiritual Warfare". Please note that the mouth or the voice is used to activate each of the weapons for use against the enemy.

EMOTIONS:

The experience of the new birth does not save or sanctify the mind or the emotions. The emotions, as with the thought life, must be submitted to the process of sanctification, that is, speaking the Word of God to the thoughts and emotions of one's soul. The emotions have been accustomed to "going their own way", and must be retrained, reigned in. The relationships and Christian service of the Christian are too important to be determined by the emotions.

THE WILL:

The Bible gives us the example of Jesus as He prayed in the garden just before His arrest, trial, and crucifixion. He prayed, "...if it be possible, let this cup pass from me, nevertheless, not my will but Your will be done." *Luke 22:42 NKJV*

Knowing full well exactly what He was facing, Jesus went through the difficulty of conforming His will to the will of the Father. Christians will have many opportunities in their life and service to the Lord to do the same, that is, to conform to the will of God.

BODY: Soma— (Greek word)—body—Strong's # 4983 BODY--EARTHLY HOUSE:₃₄

Your body is your house in which the "real you" lives while on Earth. For the Christian, when his/her earthly house (body) dies, the real person (his/her spirit and soul) immediately moves into the visible presence of God.

2 Corinthians 5:1: "For we know that if the tent which is our earthly home is destroyed, we have from God a building, a house not made with hands, eternal in the heavens." *NKJV*

2 Corinthians 5:6-8: "So we are always confident, knowing that while we are at home in the body, we are absent from the Lord. For we walk by faith, not by sight. We are confident, yes well pleased, rather to be absent from the body and to be present with the Lord."
NKJV

SUMMARY OF ENTIRE SANCTIFICATION: SPIRIT, SOUL, AND BODY:

The spirit of man must be born again, the nature changed from sin nature to righteousness, and the process of sanctification continued as God allows the believer to share in His very nature.

The soul must be transformed, the mind must be renewed, the emotions must be retrained, and the will must conform to the will of God.

The body must be presented to God as a living sacrifice, holy, acceptable to God.

WORKS CITED

1   Dorsey, Thomas A. 1988. *"The Best of the Trade" Great Gospel Songs of Thomas A Dorsey.* Hal Leonard Corp.

2   Strong, James. 2010 *Strong's Exhaustive Concordance.* Nashville, TN: Thomas Nelson Publishers, Inc. p 35 in Greek Dictionary, #1432.

3   Strong, James. 2010. *Strong's Exhaustive Concordance.* Nashville, TN: Thomas Nelson Publishers, Inc. p 72 in Greek Dictionary, #4154.

4   Taylor, Jack. 1977. *Crucifying the Old Man Lecture.* Guymon, OK: Panhandle Bible Center.

5   Strong, James. 2010. *Strong's Exhaustive Concordance.* Nashville, TN: Thomas Nelson Publishers, Inc. p 23 in Hebrew Dictionary, #1285.

6   Strong, James. 2010. *Strong's Exhaustive Concordance.* Nashville, TN: Thomas Nelson Publishers, Inc. p 22 in Greek Dictionary, #1242.

7   https://twelvetribes.org/articles/blood-covenants.

8   Strong, James 2010. *Strong's Exhaustive Concordance.* Nashville, TN: Thomas Nelson Publishers, Inc. p 46 in Greek Dictionary, #2616.

9   https://www.ncbi.nlm.nih.gov/sars-cov-2/

10 Crouch, Andre, *Broken Vessel,* Manna Music, Inc., 1968.

11 Strong, James.2010. *Strong's Exhaustive Concordance.* Nashville, TN: Thomas Nelson Publishers, Inc. p 15 in Greek Dictionary, #2616.

12 Ingles, David. 2009. *More Than Enough.* David Ingles Productions.

13 https://www.healthline.com/health/loneliness-and-depression.

14 Strong, James. 2010. *Strong's Exhaustive Concordance.* Nashville, TN: Thomas Nelson Publishers, Inc. p 100 in Greek Dictionary, #5590.

15 Strong, James. 2010. *Strong's Exhaustive Concordance.* Nashville, TN: Thomas Nelson Publishers, Inc. p 2 in Greek Dictionary, #86.

16 Strong, James. 2010. *Strong's Exhaustive Concordance.* Nashville, TN: Thomas Nelson Publishers, Inc. p 19 in Greek Dictionary, #1067.

17 Young, Robert. 1862. *Young's Literal Translation*. Grand Rapids: A Fullerton & Co.
18 Hammond, Frank & Ida Mae. 1983. *Patterns of Rejection lecture*. Houston: Faith West Church.
19 https://www.webmd.com/balance/normal-grieving-and-stages-of-grief#1.
20 Strong, James. 2010. *Strong's Exhaustive Concordance*. Nashville, TN: Thomas Nelson Publishers, Inc. p 3 in Greek Dictionary, #166.
21 Gothard, Bill. 1974. *Basic Youth Conflicts*. Oak Brook, IL: Institute in Basic Youth Conflicts.
22 https%3A%2F%2FChristian+Encyclopedia+on+legalism&oq.
23 Strong, James. 2010. *Strong's Exhaustive Concordance*. Nashville, TN: Thomas Nelson Publishers, Inc. p 51 in Greek Dictionary, #2919.
24 Strong, James. 2010. *Strong's Exhaustive Concordance*. Nashville, TN: Thomas Nelson Publishers, Inc. p 22 in Greek Dictionary, #1252.
25 Strong, James. 2010. *Strong's Exhaustive Concordance*. Nashville, TN: Thomas Nelson Publishers, Inc. p 54 in Greek Dictionary, #3056.
26 Strong, James. 2010. *Strong's Exhaustive Concordance*. Nashville, TN: Thomas Nelson Publishers, Inc. p 87 in Greek Dictionary, #4487.
27 Strong, James. 2010. *Strong's Exhaustive Concordance*. Nashville, TN: Thomas Nelson Publishers, Inc. p 56 in Greek Dictionary, #3306.
28 https://www.ancient.eu/Roman_Triumph/
29 Reidt, Wilford H. 1981. *Jesus, God's Way of Healing & Power to Promote Health: Featuring the Miracle Ministry of Dr. John G. Lake*. Tulsa, OK: Harrison House.
30 Lister, Mosie. 1958. *Till the Storm Passes By*. Mosie Lister Publishing Co.
31 Strong, James. 2010. *Strong's Exhaustive Concordance*. Nashville, TN: Thomas Nelson Publishers, Inc. p 10 in Greek Dictionary, #553.
32 Strong, James. 2010. *Strong's Exhaustive Concordance*. Nashville, TN: Thomas Nelson Publishers, Inc. p 72 in Greek Dictionary, #4151.
33 Strong, James. 2010. *Strong's Exhaustive Concordance*. Nashville, TN: Thomas Nelson Publishers, Inc. p 100 in Greek Dictionary, #5590.
34 Strong, James. 2010. Strong's Exhaustive Concordance. Nashville, TN: Thomas Nelson Publishers, Inc. p 88 in Greek Dictionary, # 4983.

BIBLIOGRAPHY FOR ARTWORK

Exc 1. Rhonda Lettow, "My Sins For His Remission of Sins", Lake of the Ozarks, MO.

Exc 2. Rhonda Lettow, "My Sin Nature For His Righteousness", Lake of the Ozarks, MO.

Exc 3. Ryan Elizabeth Ketcher, "My Spiritual Death For His Spiritual Life", Bixby, OK.

Exc 4. Ryan Elizabeth Ketcher, "My Sins as a Christian For His Forgiveness", Bixby, OK.

Exc 5. Rhonda Lettow, "My Curse for His Blessing", Lake of the Ozarks, MO.

Exc 6. Ryan Elizabeth Ketcher, "My Old Man For His New Man", Bixby, OK.

Exc 7. Ryan Elizabeth ketcher, "My Sickness For His Healing". Bixby, OK.

Exc 8. Rhonda Lettow, "My Religious Rules For His Grace", Lake of the Ozarks, MO.

Exc 9. Ryan Elizabeth Ketcher, "My Depression For His Garment of Praise", Bixby, OK.

Exc 10. Rhonda Lettow, "My Oppression For His Liberty", Lake of the Ozarks, MO.

Exc 11. Rhonda Lettow, "My emotional hurts For His Healing", Lake of the Ozarks, MO.

Exc 12. Ryan Elizabeth Ketcher, "My Stress For His Peace," Bixby, OK

Exc 13. Rhonda Lettow, "My Broken Life For His Beauty", Lake of the Ozarks, MO.

Exc 14. Ryan Elizabeth Ketcher, "My Lack For His Abundance", Bixby, OK.

Exc 15. Ryan Elizabeth Ketcher, "My Fear For His Healthy Mind", Bixby, OK.

Exc 16. Rhonda Lettow, "My Loneliness For His Constant Fellowship", Lake of the Ozarks, MO.

Exc 17. Rhonda Lettow, "My Conformity For His Transformation", Lake of the Ozarks, MO.

Exc 18. Ryan Elizabeth Ketcher, "My Poverty For His Riches", Bixby, OK.

Exc 19. Shutterstock_575573044, "My Sentence to Hades For His Promise of Heaven." (by permission-Unlimited Shutterstock License).

Exc 20. Ryan Elizabeth Ketcher, "My Rejection For His Acceptance", Bixby, OK.

Exc 21. Shutterstock_650367397.jpg, "My Grief For His Oil of Joy." (by permission-Unlimited Shutterstock License).

Exc 22. Rhonda Lettow, "My Chains of Bondage For His Freedom", Lake of the Ozarks, MO.

Exc 23. Rhonda Lettow, "My Temporal Desires For His Eternal Promises", Lake of the Ozarks, MO.

Exc 24. Rhonda Lettow, "My Condemnation For His Freedom In Christ," Lake of the Ozarks, MO.

Exc 25. Rhonda Lettow, "My Lack of Knowledge For His Discernment", Lake of the Ozarks, MO.

Exc 26. Shutterstock_631187453, "My Defeat For His Victory", (by permission). (Unlimited-Shutterstock License).

Exc 27. Shutterstock_1637179108.jpg, "Vain Imaginations For His Spiritual Weapons." (by permission-Unlimited Shutterstock License).

Exc 28. Ryan Elizabeth Ketcher, "My Weakness For His Power", Bixby, OK.

Exc 29. Shutterstock_521314966, "My Judgmentalism For His Discernment", Lake of the Ozarks, MO. (by permission-Unlimited Shutterstock License).

Exc 30. Rhonda Lettow, "My Unhealthiness For His Health", Lake of the Ozarks, MO.

Exc 31. Shutterstock_1553763224, "My Vulnerability For His Protection." (by permission-Unlimited Shutterstock License).

Exc 32. Ryan Elizabeth Ketcher, "My Darkness For His Light". Bixby, OK.

Exc 33. Rhonda Lettow, "My Weariness For His Rest", Lake of the Ozarks, MO.

SOURCES

Ancient History Encyclopedia

Amplified Version

Basic Youth Conflicts

Christian Encyclopedia

Jesus, God's Way of Healing & Power to Promote Health

King James Version

National Institute of Health

New International Version

New King James Version

Psychology Today

Seminar Notes from Jack Taylor, *Crucifying the Old Man* lecture

Seminar Notes from Bill Gothard, *Basic Youth Conflicts* lecture

Seminar Notes from Frank Hammond, Patterns of *Rejection* lecture

Shutterstock

Strong's Exhaustive Concordance

26 Translations of the New Testament

Young's Analytical Concordance

Young's Literal Translation